THE BEAUTY OF SE

J.R. Miller

Chapter 1

The Beauty of Self-Control

All of life should be beautiful. God is a God of beauty. He never made anything that was not beautiful. Paul, in designating certain qualities of character which every Christian should strive to attain, names "whatever things are *lovely*." Nothing that is unlovely should be allowed in the life of any Christian. We should always strive to be beautiful in life. Marden names as signs of deterioration in character, "when you are *satisfied with mediocrity*, when *commonness* does not trouble you, when a slighted job does not haunt you."

Self-control is one of the finest things in any life. It is not a single element in character—but something that has to do with all the element. It binds them all together in one. In one of Paul's clusters of the qualities of a noble character, he names—love, joy, peace, patience, kindness, goodness, faithfulness, meekness, ending with *self-control*. Self-control is self-mastery. It is kingship over all life. At the center of your being, sits yourself. Your seat ought to be a throne. If you are not in control, if there are any forces in your nature which are unruly, which do not acknowledge your sway—you are not the king which you should be. Part of your kingdom is in insurrection. The strength of your life is divided. The strong man is he whose whole being is subject to him.

Perfect self-control is ideal life. You are like a man driving a team of spirited horses. So long as he sits on the driver's set and the horses obey him implicitly, acknowledging the slightest pressure upon the reins—all is well. But if the animals become ungovernable, begin to chomp on the bits, and cease to obey the driver's impulse, and then dash away from his guidance—he has lost his control. *A man has self-control when he sits in his place—and has his hands on all the reins of his life.* His is kingly when he has complete master of his *temper*, his *speech*, his *feelings*, his *appetites*; when he can be quiet under injury and wrong; deeply hurt but showing no sign of malice; patient and still under severe provocation; when he can stand amid *temptations* and not yield to them.

A man when *insulted* may break out into a passion of anger, and become a very "son of thunder" in the vehemence of his rage. But that is not strength. The man who when treated unjustly remains silent, answers not a word, with cheeks white, yet restraining himself, showing no resentment—but keeping love in his heart—is the strong man. The Wise Man puts it thus: "He who is slow to anger—is better than the mighty; and he who rules his spirit—is better than he who takes a city."

There are men who rule *other* men—but cannot rule *themselves*. They are victorious in battle—but they cannot control their own temper, restrain their own speech, or calm and quiet their own hearts. There is nothing beautiful in such a life. Nothing more effectually mars a life—than fretfulness, discontent, worry, or impatience. Nothing is more pitiful—than a life which is made to be strong, kingly, noble, calm, and peaceful—but which is, instead, the slave of every excitement, every temper, every resentment, every appetite and passion. Someone says, "Alexander conquered all the world—except Alexander."

Not only is self-control strong — it is also beautiful. Anger is not beautiful. Ungoverned temper is not lovely. Rage is demonic. But a spirit calm, strong, and unflustered, amid storms of feeling and all manner of disturbing emotions—is sublime in its beauty. "A temper under control, a heart subdued into tenderness and patience, a voice cheerful with hope, and a countenance bright with kindness—are invaluable possessions to any man or woman."

The Bible furnishes examples of self-control. One is in the story of King Saul's anointing. The people received him with great enthusiasm. "All the people shouted, and said, Long live the King." He then went to his house, and the army went with him. But there were a few who refused to accept him. "Certain worthless fellows said, how shall this man save us? And they despised him, and brought him no present." Saul might have resented the insult offered him, for he was king now, and might have slain those who refused to receive him; but he restrained himself and spoke not a word. Amid the sneers and scoffs of these worthless men, he was as though he heard nothing of all they said. He held his peace.

We are apt to *resent* insults, and *retaliate* when others do us evil. But the Christian way is either not to speak at all, or to give the soft answer which turns away wrath. *The way to conquer an enemy—is to treat him with kindness!* Ignoring slights and quietly going on with love's duty, returning kindness for unkindness, is the way to get the true victory. The best answer to sneers, scoffs, and abuse—is a life of persistent patience and gentleness.

It is in **Jesus** that we have the finest illustrations of self-control, as of all noble qualities. The tongue is the hardest of all the members of the body to control. No man can tame it, says James. Yet Jesus had perfect mastery over his tongue. He never said a word that he would better not have said. He never spoke unadvisedly. When bitterly assailed by enemies, when they sought to catch him in his words, when they tried by false accusations to make him speak angrily—he held his peace and said not a word. Not only did he refrain from hasty and ill tempered speech— but he kept his heart in control. Some men can keep silence with their lips though in their hearts the fire burns hotly; but Jesus kept love in his heart under all provocation. He was master of his thoughts and feelings. He never grew angry or bitter. When he was reviled—he did not revile in return; when he was hated—he loved on; when nails were driven through his hands—the blood from his wounds became the blood of redemption!

Nor was it *weakness* in Jesus, which kept him silent under men's reproaches and reviling, and under all injuries and insults. There was no moment when he could not have summoned legions of angels to defend him and to strike down his persecutors. He voluntarily accepted wrong—when he could have resisted. He never lifted a finger on his own behalf, though he could have crushed his enemies. He returned *kindness* for *unkindness*. Thus he set us the example of patient endurance of wrong, of silent suffering, rather than angry retaliation.

In his *words*, also, Christ teaches us this lesson of self-control. Meekness is one of the Beatitudes. It is the ripe fruit of restraint, under insult and wrong. "Accustom yourself to injustice" was the counsel of an English preacher. It is not easy to accept such teaching. We do not like to be treated unjustly. We can learn to endure a good many other things—and still keep patient and sweet. But to endure injustice seems to be beyond the "seventy times seven" included in our Lord's measurement of forgiving. Yet it is not beyond the limit of *the law of love*. Certainly the Master in his own life accustomed himself to injustice. He was silent even under the worst injustices, and he leaves the lesson of his example to us.

The beauty of self-control! It is always *beautiful*, and the lack of it is always a *blemish*. A lovely face which has won us by its beauty, instantly loses its charm and winsomeness, when in some excitement, bad temper breaks out. An angry countenance is disfiguring. It hides the *angel* and reveals the *demon*. Self-control gives calmness and poise. It should be practiced not only on great occasions—but on the smallest. A hundred times a day it will save us from *weakness* and *fluster*—and make us *strong* a *quiet*. It is the outcome of peace. If the heart is still and quiet with the peace of Christ—the whole life is under heavenly guard. The *king* is on his throne—and there is no misrule anywhere.

How can we get this self-control which means so much to our lives? It is essential if we would live beautifully. We are weak without it. *How can we get the mastery over ourselves?* It is not attained by a mere *resolve*. We cannot simply assert our self-mastery, and then have it. We cannot put self-control on the throne, by a mere proclamation. It is an achievement which must be won by ourselves, and won by degrees. It is a lesson which must be learned, a long lesson which it takes many days to learn. As Lowell says:

"Beauty and truth and all that these contain,
Drop not like ripened fruit about our feet;
We climb to them through years of sweat and pain."

We need *divine* help in learning the lesson. Yet we must be *diligent* in doing our part. God helps those who help themselves. When we strive to be calm and self-controlled, he puts his own strength into our heart. Then we shall find ourselves growing strong and gaining in self-mastery. The attainment will come slowly.

But however long it may take us to reach this heavenly achievement, we should never be content until we have reached it. This is the sum of all learning and experience. It is the completeness of all spiritual culture. The man in us is only part a man—while we are not master of ourselves. We are in grave peril while any weak hour we may lose our kingliness and be cast down. It took Moses forty years to learn self-control—and he did not learn it in the world's universities; it was only when God was his teacher and his school was in the desert, that he mastered it.

Then in a sad, unwatched moment he lost his kingly power for an instant and spoke a few words unadvisedly, and failed and could not finish his work!

Think what the lack of self-control is costing men continually! One moment's dropping of the *reins*—and a wrong decision is made—a temptation is accepted—a battle is lost—and a splendid life lies in ruin! Let us achieve the grace of self-control.

Chapter 2

The Work of the Plough

The figure of *ploughing*, much used in the Bible, is very suggestive.
The *initial* work in making *Christians*—is plough work. Human hearts are hard, and the first tool which must go over them, must be a plough, that they may be broken up and softened. In our Lord's parable, some seeds fell on the trodden wayside. The soil was good—it was the same as that which, in another part of the field, yielded a hundredfold—but it was hard. It had been long a roadway across the field and thousands of feet had gone over it, treading it down. There was no use in sowing seed upon it, for the ground would not receive it, and lying upon the hardened surface, the birds in eager quest for food would pick it off. The only way to make anything of this trodden roadside, was to have it broken up by the plough.

The first work of Christ in many lives is ploughing. The lives have not been cultivated. They have been left untilled. Or, like the wayside ground, they have been trodden down into hardness. Many people treat their lives as if they were meant to be open commons, instead of beautiful gardens. They do not fence them in to protect them—and so beasts pasture on them, trampling over them; children play upon them; and men drive their carriages and their heavy wagons across them making roadways as hard as rock. We readily understand this in *agriculture*, and it is little more difficult to understand it in *life* culture.

A godly woman said that God wanted her heart to be a garden filled with sweet flowers. A *garden* needs constant care. Our lives should be watched continually, that the soil shall always be tender, so that all manner of lovely things may grow in them—but there are many lives that are not thus cared for and cultivated. They are unfenced, and all kinds of harsh feet go treading over them. No care is given to the companions who are allowed admittance into the field; soon the gentle things are destroyed, and the tender, mellow soil has become hard. Those who are entrusted with the care of children should never fail to think of their responsibility for the influences which are allowed to touch them.

For the lack of such care, many men and women become hardened, without capacity to receive tender impressions. They have large capacities for rich, beautiful life and for splendid service—but they are permitted to read all kinds of *books,* and to have all kinds of *amusements,* and to see all kinds of *entertainments*, and to see all kinds of evil life—and they grow up without beauty, really useless and without loveliness. They need to be ploughed and ploughed deep, that they may be made fertile.

God himself does a great deal of ploughing. His **Word** is a plough. It cuts its way into men's lives, crushing the heart, revealing sinfulness, producing penitence. It finds men impenitent—and leaves them broken and contrite, confessing sin and asking for mercy. David tells us, in one of his penitential Psalms, how he tried for a long time to hide his sins—but how his pain became unbearable, until he confessed. God's plough went deep into his heart. Then when at length he confessed his sin, forgiveness came and peace and joy. David became a new man after that. God's Spirit had ploughed up his heart.

A Bible found its way into a home where a Bible had never been before. The man of the house began to read it aloud to his wife in the evenings, and the words entered their hearts. One night, after reading aloud portions of the book, the man said, "Wife, if this book is true—then we are *wrong*." The book condemned them. They became troubled. The word was ploughing its way in their hearts. Next evening, as they read again, the sense of sin in them became still deeper, and the man said, "Wife, if this book is true—then we are *lost*." They became very greatly distressed. The words they had read had shown them that they were sinners, guilty, and lost. Next night they read again, and found something of hope—they had read of divine love and mercy, and the man said, "Wife, if this book is true—then we can be saved." The word of God does mighty plough work in men's hearts before they can be made fruitful.

Sorrow ofttimes is God's plough. We dread pain and shrink from it. It seems destructive and ruinous. The plough tears its way, with its keen, sharp blade, through our hearts—and we say we are being destroyed! When the process is completed and we look upon the garden with its sweet flowers growing—we see that only blessing, enrichment, and beauty are the result. We complain of our suffering, but we cannot afford to have suffering taken away.

We cannot afford to lose pain out of the *world*—or out of our *life*. It means too much to us. We owe too much, get too many joys and treasures from it—to have it taken out of our lives. We owe to suffering many of the treasures of experience. Without pain we never could know Christ deeply, intimately, experimentally. Two friends may love each other very sincerely, without suffering together—but it is a new friendship into which they enter when they stand side by side in a great sorrow. Grief reveals Christ and draws him closer to us, and we love him better afterwards. To take pain from the world would be to rob life of its divinest joy, it richest blessings. If the plough never cut through the soil—there would be no furrows and no golden harvests.

This plough work is for every one of us. God is making us—and that is the way he has to do it. A little child had a garden, which her father had given her. But nothing would grow in it. The flowers and plants would begin to come up—but in a short time they would wither and die. She had little pleasure from her garden. One day her father brought some workmen with heavy iron tools, and they began to tear up her garden. The removed the soil. They destroyed everything beautiful in it. The child begged that the men would go away. She said they were ruining her garden. But they heeded not her imploring and tears. They broke up the ground and found a great rock just below the surface. This they took away, then smoothed down the soil, and made it beautiful again. After that the flowers and plants grew into beauty. Then the child understood the value of the plough work, which at first seemed so destructive—but in the end left her garden a place of rare beauty.

Christ has, in his love for us—a wonderful vision of what he wants us to become. He would have us share his own glory. "Let the beauty of the Lord our God be upon us" is a prayer God loves to answer. He wants us to become radiant in loveliness. He wants love to blossom in our lives into all gentleness, sweetness, purity, and patience, into ideal manliness, heroic nobleness, splendid sacrificial life. But we never can attain this vision in ways of *ease*. To spare us from the pain, struggle and suffering—is not the way of truest kindness for us. It needs the plough and sharp plough-work, to bring us to our best beauty.

Ploughing is hard work. It is hard for him who follows the plough through the long furrows. There seems to be no reward for him. It is all painful work that he does—cutting and crushing the soil. He sees no growing seed, no golden harvest. It is all weariness, aches and toil for him, with nothing to cheer his heart, nothing to enrich him. The reaper rejoices as he thrusts in his sickle and then threshes out the yellow grain. But the work of the ploughman seems to be *destruction* for the time. Yet in the end it proves to be glorious work.

It is hard also for the soil, to have the plough of God driven through our hearts and over our lives, breaking them and crushing them. Oh, how heavy God's plough is, as it is dragged over us, its sharp plow-share cutting into the very center of our being. Rough is the plough work. It has no comfort in it. No reward is apparent. The plough cuts remorselessly. But the ploughman may have visions of a rich outcome from all his toil. There will be a harvest by and by, when, in the place where his share now cuts, golden grain will wave, and he will fill his bosom with sheaves. You cry out today because of the pain you suffer as God's plough cuts into your life and seems to be spoiling all its beauty. But look forward. First the plough—then the fields with their glorious grain. Now you know nothing but pain; hereafter you will reap joy from the places now scarred and furrowed.

There is a picture in Revelation which explains it all. There appeared a great company, wearing white robes and carrying palm branches. "Who are these?" was asked. "These are those who have come out of the great tribulation," was the answer. The way to heaven's highest glory—lies through pain. Today the plough is cutting through your life; tomorrow a blessed harvest will wave!

Chapter 3

Finding Our Duties

Some people have trouble in discovering God's guidance in everyday life. Perhaps the trouble is that they look for the direction in some unusual way, whereas, ordinarily, it is shown to them very simply.

Duty never is a haphazard thing. There never are a half dozen things any one of which we may fitly do at any particular time; there is some one definite thing in the divine thought for each moment. In writing music, no composer strews the notes along the staff just as they happen to fall on this line or that space; he sets them in harmonious order and succession, so that they will make sweet music when played or sung. The builder does not fling the beams or stones into the edifice without plan; every block of wood, or stone, or iron, and every brick have its place, and the building rises in graceful beauty.

The days are like the lines and spaces in the musical staff, and duties are the notes; each life is meant to make a harmony and in order to do this, each single duty must have its own proper place. One thing done out of its time and place makes discord in the music of life, just as one note misplaced on the musical staff makes discord. Each life is a building, and the little acts are the materials used; the whole is congruous and beautiful only when every act is in its own true place.

The art of true living therefore, consists largely in doing always those things which belongs to the moment. But to know what is the duty of each moment is the question which, to, many people is full of perplexity. Yet it would be easy if our obedience were but more simple. We have only to take the duty which comes next to our hand. Our duty never is some far away thing. We do not have to search for it—but it is always close at hand and easily found. The trouble is that we complicate the question of duty for ourselves by our way of looking at life, and then get our feet entangled in the meshes which our own hands have woven.

Much of this confusion arises from taking *too long views*. We try to settle our duty in long sections. We think of years rather than of moments, of a whole life work rather than of individual acts. It is hard to plan a year's duty; it is easy to plan just for one short day. No shoulder can bear up the burden of a year's cares, all gathered into one load—but the weakest shoulder can carry without weariness what really belongs to one little day. In trying to grasp the whole year's work, we are apt to overlook and to miss that of the present hour, just as one, in gazing at a far off mountain top, is likely not to see the little flower blooming at his feet, and even tread it down as he stumbles along.

There is another way in which people complicate the question of duty. They try to reach decisions today, on matters which really are not before them today, and which will not be before them for months—but possibly for years. For example, a young man came to his pastor in very sore perplexity over a question of duty. He said he could not decide whether he ought to go as a foreign missionary or devote his life to work in some home field. Yet the young man had only closed his freshman year at college. It would require him three years more to complete his college course, and then he would have to spend three years in a theological seminary. Six years hence he would be ready for his work as a minister, and it was concerning his choice of field then that the young man was now in such perplexity. He said that often he passed hours on his knees at prayer, seeking for light—but no light had come. He had even tried fasting—but without avail. The matter had so taken possession of his mind that he had scarcely been able to study during the last term, and he had fallen behind in his classes. His health, too, he felt, was being endangered, as he often lay awake much of the night, thinking about the momentous question of his duty, as between home and foreign work.

It is very easy to see what this young man's mistake was—he was trying to settle now a question with which he had nothing whatever to do at the present time. If he is spared to complete his course of training, the question will emerge as a really practical one, several years hence. It is folly *now* to compel a decision which he cannot make intelligently and without perplexity. It is very evident therefore that this decision is no part of his present duty. He wonders that he can get no light on the matter—but that even in answer to agonizing prayer, the perplexity does not grow less. But is there any ground to expect God to throw light on a man's path so far in advance? Is there any promise that prayer for guidance at a point so remote should be answered today? Why should it be? Will it not be time enough for the answer to come when the decision must really be made?

It is right, no doubt, for the young man to pray about the matter—but his present request should be that God would direct his preparation, so that he may be fitted for the work, whatever it may be, that in the divine purpose is waiting for him, and that, at the proper time, God would lead him to his allotted field. "Lord, prepare me for what you are preparing for me," was the daily prayer of one young life. This would have been a fitting prayer for this young student; but to pray that he may know where the Lord will send him to labor when he is ready, six years hence, is certainly an unwarranted asking which is little short of presumption and of impertinent human intermeddling with divine things.

Another obvious element of mistake in this man's case is that he is neglecting his present duty, or failing to do it well, while he is perplexing himself with what his duty will be years hence. Thus he is hindering the divine purpose in the work his Master has planned for him. *Life is not an hour too long. It requires every moment of our time to work out the divine plan for our lives.* The preparatory years are enough, if they are faithfully used, in which to prepare for the years of life work which come after. But every hour we waste, leaves its own flaw in the preparation. Many people go halting and stumbling all through their later years, missing opportunities, and continually failing where they ought to have succeeded, because they neglected their duty in the preparatory years. There are more people who, like this student, worry about matters that belong altogether to the future, than there are those who are anxious to do well the duty for the present moment. *If we would simply do always the next thing, we would be relieved of all perplexity.*

The law of divine guidance is, step by step. One who carries a lantern on a country road at night, sees only one step before him. If he takes that step, however, he carries his lantern forward and this makes another step plain. At length he reaches his destination without once stepping into the darkness. The whole way has been made light for him, though only a step at a time. This is the usual method of God's guidance. The Bible is represented as a lamp unto the feet. It is a lamp, or lantern—but not a blazing sun, nor even a lighthouse—but a plain, common lantern, which one can carry about in his hand. It is a lamp unto the feet, not throwing its beams afar, not illumining a whole hemisphere—but shining only on the bit of road on which the pilgrim's feet are walking.

If this is the way God guides us, it ought never to be hard for us to find our duty. It never lies far away, inaccessible to us, it is always "the next thing." It never lies out of sight, in the darkness, for God never puts our duty where we cannot see it. The thing we think may be our duty—but which is still lying in obscurity, is not yet our duty, whatever it may be a little farther on. The duty for the moment is always perfectly clear—and that is as far as we need concern ourselves. When we do the little which is plain to us, we will carry the light on, and it will shine on the next moment's step.

If not even one little step of duty is plain to us, "the next thing" is to *wait* a little. Sometimes that is God's will for us for the moment. At least, it never is his will that we should take a step into the darkness. He never hurries us. We had better always wait than rush on as if we were not quite sure of the way. Often, in our impatience, we do hasten things, which we find after a little while, were not God's next things for us at all. That was Peter's mistake when he cut off a man's ear in the Garden, and it led to sore trouble and humiliation a little later. There are many quick, impulsive people, who are continually doing *wrong next things*, and who then find their next thing trying to undo the last. We should always wait for God, and should never take a step which he has not made light for us.

Yet we must not be too slow. This is as great a danger as being too quick. The people of Israel were never to march until the pillar moved—but they were neither to run ahead nor to lag behind God. *Indolence* is as bad as *rashness*. Being too late is as bad as being too soon. There are some people who are never on time. They never do things just when they ought to be done. They are continually in perplexity which of several things they ought to do first. The trouble is, they are forever putting off or neglecting or forgetting things, and consequently each morning finds them not only facing that day's duties—but the omitted duties of past days as well. There never really are two duties for the same moment, and if everything is done in its own time, there never will be any perplexity about what special right thing to do next.

It is an immeasurable comfort that our duties are not the accidents of any undirected flow of circumstances. We are clearly assured that if we acknowledge the Lord in all our ways, he will direct our paths. "Trust in the Lord with all your heart, and do not rely on your own understanding; in all your ways acknowledge Him, and He will guide you on the right paths." Proverbs 3:5-6. That is, if we keep eye and heart ever turned toward God, we never shall be left to grope after the path, for it will be made plain to us. We are authorized to pray that God would order our steps. What direction in duty could be minuter than this? "He who follows me *shall* not walk in the darkness," said the Master (John 8:12). "He who follows me." We must not run on ahead of him, neither must we lag behind; in either case we shall find darkness, just as deep darkness in advance of our Guide, if we will not wait for him, as it is behind him, if we will not keep close up to him.

Prompt, unquestioning, undoubting following of Christ—takes all perplexity out of Christian life, and gives unbroken peace. There is something for every moment, and duty is always "the next thing." It may sometimes be an interruption, setting aside a cherished plan of our own, breaking into a pleasant rest we had arranged, or taking us away from some favorite occupation. It may be to meet a disappointment, to take up a cross, to endure a sorrow or to pass through a trial. It may be to go upstairs into our room and be sick for a time, letting go our hold upon all active life. Or it may be just the plainest, commonest bit of routine work in the home, in the office, on the farm, at school.

Most of us find the greater number of our "next things" in the tasks that are the same day after day, yet even in the interstices, amid these set tasks, there come a thousand little things of kindness, patience, gentleness, thoughtfulness, obligingness, like the sweet flowers which grow in the crevices upon the cold, hard rocks—and we should be ready always for these as we hurry along, as well as for the sterner duties that our common calling brings to us.

There never is a moment without duty, and if we are living near to Christ and following him closely, we never shall be left in ignorance of what he wants us to do. If there is nothing, absolutely nothing, we can do, at any particular time, and then we may be sure that the Master wants us to rest. For he is not a hard Master, and besides, rest is as needful in its time, as work. So we must not worry when there come moments which seem to have no task for our hands. "The next thing" then, is to sit down and wait.

Chapter 4

Into the Right Hands

"Hold me up—and I shall be safe!" Psalm 119:117

Certain ancient mariners were accustomed to say, as they put out to sea, "Keep me, O God, for my boat is so small—and the ocean is so great and stormy!" There could not be a fitter prayer for a Christian—as he sets out in life. The world is vast and full of perils, and a Christian, even the best, is very weak and frail. He has no ability to face the difficulties, the obstacles, the hardships he must face, if he is to pass successfully through life. The world is large and full of storm and struggle—and only a few get through it safely.

If there were no one greater and stronger than ourselves, into whose keeping we may commit our lives, as we go out to meet the perils—what hope could we have of ever getting through safely? The Christian cannot guide himself. He cannot master the storms. He cannot shelter himself. "Keep of me safe, O God, for in You I take refuge!" (Psalm 16:1) should be his prayer, not once only when he launches his barque—but daily, hourly.

But does God really care for our little individual lives? Does he care for the child that has lost the shelter of human love, and has no one to think of it or provide for it? Does the great God give thought and care to one little child among the millions of the world?

The very thing that Jesus wants to do for us—is to be the keeper of our lives as we pass through the world with its storms and dangers. We do not know what we lose when we keep our lives out of the hands of Christ. No other can make of us what he could make. No other can bring out the powers and possibilities of our being as he can. Our lives are like musical instruments. They have marvelous capacities—but only one who has the skill can bring out the music. Only one who understands our lives, with all their strange powers, can call out their possibilities.

There is a story of an organist in one of the cities of Germany, who one day refused to permit a visitor to play upon his organ. The visitor begged to be allowed at least to put his hands upon the keys and play a few notes, and the old man reluctantly consented. The moment the stranger began to play, the organ gave forth such music as it never had given forth before. The custodian was amazed, recognizing the fact that a master was at his keys. When he asked who it was, the player answered, "I am Mendelssohn." "And I refuse you permission to play upon my organ!" the old man said, in grief and self reproach.

It is said that one day, many years ago, there was an auction in London which was attended by distinguished people. Among other things offered for sale was a Stradivarius violin, more than a hundred years old. The auctioneer raised the violin and held it gently, almost reverently, as he told its story and spoke of its wonderful qualities. Then he gave it to a musician who was present, asking him to play upon it. The man played as well as he could—but the violin in his hands failed to win enthusiasm from the audience.

The auctioneer began to call for bids. But the responses came slowly. Then a stranger came into the room, an Italian. He pressed his way to the side of the auctioneer to see the violin. He took it into his own hands, examined it carefully, held it to his ear as if it had some secret to whisper to him, and then laid it gently on his breast and began to play upon it—and marvelous music at once filled the room. The people were strangely affected. Some smiled, some wept; every heart was stirred. It was Paganini, the great master, whose fingers were on the strings. When he laid the instrument down, the bidding began again, and there was no trouble now in selling it. In the hands of the first player—the qualities of the violin were not brought out, and men did not know what a treasure was being offered to them. But in the hands of the great master—its marvelous powers were discovered and brought out.

Our lives are like violins. In the right hands they will give forth wonderful music. But in unskillful hands, their powers are not discovered. It is strange with what lack of thought and care, many people entrust their lives into the hands of those who cannot bring out the *best* that is in them—and ofttimes of those who only do them *harm*. This is seen in the recklessness which many young people show in choosing their friends. Indeed, they do not *choose* their friends at all—but let themselves drift into association and intimacy with any who come their way. The influence of **friendship** is almost irresistible. The admission of a new companion into our life is the beginning of a new epoch in our course. If the friendship is pure, inspiring, and elevating, if the friend is one who in his own character will set before us new visions of beautiful life, and in all his influence over us will prove inspiring, the day of his coming to us will ever be a day to be remembered. But if the new friend is unworthy, or if his hands are unskillful, nothing good can come from his friendship. His coming into our life is a tragedy.

Young people should seek association with those who are wiser and more experienced than themselves, those who can teach them lessons they have not yet learned, lead them in paths they have not yet walked in, and help them to find their own powers and possibilities. It is a great mistake merely to choose a friend with whom to have a good time, one who will flatter us and make us feel satisfied with ourselves, one with whom we may get on pleasantly. We should have friends who, like Paganini with the Cremona, can discover and call out the best that is in us. "Our best friend is he who makes us do what we can."

It is the same with the **teachers** to whom we may go. There are those who have wisdom enough to teach, and who honestly do the best they can with those who come to them—but who lack the mental vision to discover the faculties that are in their pupils, or who lack the ability and skill to bring out their possibilities. There are other teachers who may know less themselves—but they have the power to find the talents that are in their pupils, and then to call them out.

The same is true of the value and influence of **books**. There are books which we may enjoy reading, and which may give us entertainment and pleasure—but which leave in our minds no new knowledge, no stimulating of thought, no new visions of beauty, no wonder to impel us to advance, and no strengthening of character. On the other hand, there are books which stir our hearts, which wake us up, which kindle in us upward inspirations, and which incite us to the attaining of better things. These are the books we should read, for they will give us the help we most need if we are to grow into fullness of life and power.

But whoever or whatever we may take into our life—**Christ should always have the first place as Master, Guide, and Friend**. No other one knows the capacities that are in us, and no other can find and bring out these capacities and train them for the highest service. Into Christ's hands, therefore, we should commit our lives for teaching, for discipline, for the developing of their powers. Then we shall reach our best, and realize the divine thought for us.

Christ alone, is able to **keep** our lives. He is the Master of all the world. He met every power and conquered it. He faced all evil and overcame it. We never can find ourselves in the hands of any enemy, who is too strong for him. One of the most beautiful ascriptions in the Bible is that which says: "To Him who is able to keep you from falling and to present you before His glorious presence without fault and with great joy—to the only God our Savior be glory, majesty, power and authority, through Jesus Christ our Lord, before all ages, now and forevermore!" In all this world's dangers, he can guard our lives from harm, and he can present us at last without blemish.

Christ alone, is able to **guide** us. The world is a great mass of tangled paths. They run everywhere, crossing each other in all directions. Hands are forever beckoning us here and there, and we know not which beckoning to follow. Even *friendship*, loyal as it may be, sincere and sympathetic as it is, lacks wisdom and may guide us mistakenly. There is One only whose wisdom is infallible, whose advice never errs—and he is our Guide. There is a little prayer in one of the Psalms which pleads: "Let the morning bring me word of your unfailing love, for I have put my trust in you. Show me the way I should go, for to you I lift up my soul." Psalms 143:8. This prayer, if sincere, will always be answered. We may see no hand leading us. We may hear no voice saying, as we walk in the darkness, "This is the way—walk in it." Yet if we seek divine guidance and accept it implicitly, we shall always have it.

Not only do we have keeping and guidance in Christ—but everything we need on the way—and then eternal blessedness! We may commit our lives into His hands with absolute confidence. He will take us with all our faults and our sins—and will keep us from hurt in all the perils of the way. He will lead us in the right path amid all the confusion and tangle—and then He will then bring us to glory!

Chapter 5

Living Unto God

"Settle it in your heart that the sum of all business and blessedness, is to live to God." John Wesley

"The glory is not in the task—but in doing it for Him." Jean Ingelow

The *object* of our life determines its character. What we live for—tells what we are. If a man's aim is to get rich, if that is the ruling motive of his life—greed for gold is his absorbing passion. If a man lives to do good to his fellow men, if this is his single purpose, the desire will inspire all his thoughts and actions.

It is interesting to put ourselves to the test to discover just what the real purpose of our living is. When we know this we can tell where our life is tending, what it will be when it is finished, what impression we are making on the world, and what our living means to God.

That which distinguishes a Christian life from others—is that it is God's. We belong to God. To live to any other, therefore, is disloyalty and idolatry. Paul in one of his epistles, asserts this truth very strongly. He says, "None of us lives to himself, and none dies to himself. For whether we live—we live unto the Lord; or whether we die—we die unto the Lord; whether we liver therefore, or die—we are the Lord's."

All our relations are with the Lord. To him we owe our full obedience—we have no other master. It is his work we are doing, whether it be what we call *secular* work, or whether it be what we consider *religious* work. In all our acts, words, thoughts, feelings—we are living to the Lord—if we are living worthily. We may not be conscious of this relation—but whether we are or not, it is to the Lord that we are living. We may not think definitely of God every time we speak, every time we do anything—but if we are sincere our desire always is to please God, to honor him, to have his approval. It is to the Lord that we must answer in judgment. "We shall all stand before the judgment seat of God—each one of us shall give account of himself to God."

The truest life, is that which is lived most fully and unbrokenly unto God. Jenny Lind said, in accounting for the motive and spirit of her wonderful singing, *"I sing to God."* She meant that she looked into God's face, as it were, and consciously sang to him. She did not sing to the vast audience that hung on her words and was held spellbound by them. She was scarcely conscious of any face before her but God's. She thought of no listening ear but God's. We may not all be able to enter into such perfect relation with God as did this marvelous singer—but this is the only true ideal of all Christian life. We should do each piece of work for God.
The *business* man should do all his business for God. The *artist* should paint his picture for God. The *writer* should write his book for God. The *farmer* should until his ground for God. This means that we are always engaged in the Father's business, and must do it all in a way that he will approve.

Jesus was a carpenter, for many years working at the carpenter's bench. We are sure that he did each piece of work for his Father's eye. He did it skillfully, conscientiously, beautifully. He did not skimp it, nor hurry through it, so as to get away from the shop earlier.

What a transformation it would make in all our work if we could say in truth, *"I do it for God."* Now this is not an impossible ideal for Christian life. It was this that Paul meant, in part, at least, when he said, "To me to live *is* Christ." He was living *in* Christ. He was living *for* Christ. His life was all Christ—Christ living in him. He had the same conception of Christian life when he wrote, "Whether therefore you eat, or drink, or whatever you do—do all to the glory of God." Even our eating and drinking are included in this high ideal. The sins of gluttony and intemperance in drinking are condemned. We must also eat healthfully: eat to live— and not live to eat. To do anything to the glory of God is to do it so that it will reflect the divine glory, and be for the divine honor. This is part of what Paul meant when he said, "We live unto the Lord."

It is possible to follow the guidance of conscience in all things, doing always what is right—and yet not live unto the Lord, not to have any consciousness of God, any sense of a personal God, any thought of God at all, in what we say or do. It is possible to accept the *Christian moralities* as our rule of life, following them even in the smallest things—yet not be living unto God, not even believing in God nor having any love for him. When the singer said, "I sing to God," she meant that she thought of God as she sang, and poured forth her song directly in praise and love to him. So we should seek to do all our work for God.

There cannot but be a wonderful inspiration in living in this way unto God, if we make it real. It is not always easy to work under those who are over us. Sometimes they are unjust, unfair in their treatment of us, unkind toward us, tyrannical in their exactions of service or in their manner of enforcing their commands. It is easy for us to fret and chafe when we have to endure *severity* or *unkindness* in the performance of our daily tasks. But it changes everything, if we are conscious of another Master, in back of the human master, and remember that he is the one for whom we really are working. He is never unfair or unjust, never severe or harsh. We can work joyfully with him and for him, unaffected by the hardness or the inhumanity of the human master who is immediately over us. We may bear the harshness, the injustice, the unkindness we have to endure, if it is our duty to stay in the place, seeing ever the eye of Christ, with its love and sympathy, looking upon us and enduring all the harshness for him.

Paul exhorts servants to be obedient to their masters—"as servants of Christ, doing the will of God from the heart." "Whatever you do," he says, "work heartily, as unto the Lord, and not unto men; knowing that from the Lord you shall receive the recompense of the inheritance: you serve the Lord Christ." It makes the most trying service easy, when it is done in this way—but looking beyond the human master and *seeing* Christ as the real Master, for whom we are working. We are *living* unto him. We are *serving* him. From him we shall receive the reward for our faithfulness.

Paul speaks in this same connection of dying. It does not seem strange to hear him say, "Whether we live—we live unto the Lord." But when he goes on and says, "Whether we die—we die unto the Lord," the words strike us as unusual and startle us. Dying does not interrupt nor in any way interfere with our relations to Christ. It is just like any other passage in life. *Dying is only a phase or experience of living.* We are as really Christ's, when we die and after we die—as we are when we are living. The words are wonderfully illuminating; they throw a bright light on the mystery of dying. We are not separated from Christ in death; the bond between us and him is not broken. When we die we do not pass out of Christ's service; we only pass to another form of service. We have the impression that death cuts our life off, interrupts it, and makes an entire change in everything which concerns us. But the truth is, life goes on through death—and after death very much the same as it did before. There will be nothing greatly new in our experience, nothing strange or unusual, when we are dead. Life and death are all one—parts of the same continued existence. "Whether we live—we live unto the Lord; or whether we die—we die unto the Lord; whether we live therefore, or die—we are the Lord's."

There really is nothing to dread, therefore, in dying. The Old Testament Scriptures represent it as a walk *through the valley*, the valley of the shadow of death, accompanied by the Shepherd, whose presence allays all fear and gives peace. In the New Testament what we call dying is a departure from earth, in the companionship of Christ. There is a mystery in it because it is away from all that we know or understand and all that we can see—but there is nothing in it to be dreaded—for it does not separate from Christ for an instant—and it takes the person to Christ to be with him forever. We are to die unto the Lord, with no interruption to our attachment to him, and then continue, in the heavenly life, living unto the Lord. For life will go on with its blessed activities in heaven. Our work may differ in its character—but we shall ever be loving and serving Christ.

Thus our relation with Christ is for all time, through death, and through eternity. He does not become our Savior merely to deliver us in some emergency. Ofttimes this is all that we can do for a man who is in distress or need. We can relieve him for the time—but when the occasion is past he drops away from us, perhaps back into his old trouble, and our relation to him ceases. But when we accept Christ as our Savior it is forever. He takes us into his love and into his life. He establishes a relation with us that never shall be broken. He will never weary of us. We may sin against him— but he will not cast us off. We may be unfaithful to him and may wander far away—but when we repent and creep back to him, he will forgive us and receive us again to the place of love. The marriage covenant has a limitation, for it is "until death us do part." But there is no such limitation in the covenant made between Christ and us. Death will not part us from him. We belong to him in the heavenly life. We are to follow him in this world to the very last, and then forever in the world to come. We are to do the will of God on earth as it is done in heaven, and then continue to do his will when we reach heaven.

Chapter 6

The Indispensable Christ

One of Christ's words to his disciples was, "Without me you can do nothing." If anyone is thinking of giving up Christ, let him wait a moment and ponder the question, whether he can afford to do it or not. What will it mean to him to give up Christ? There are some losses which do not take much from us; there are some friends whom we might lose and be little the poorer. But what would it take out of our life to give up Christ? "Without me," he says, "you can do nothing."

An old writer tells of dreaming that a strange thing happened to his Bible. Every word in it that referred to Christ had faded from the pages. He turned to the New Testament to find the Gospels, and found only blank paper. He looked for the prophecies about the Messiah, which he used to read, and they all had been blotted out. He recalled sweet promises which he used to lean on with delight—but not one of them could be found. The name of Christ had faded from every place where once it had been. What would it mean to us to find ourselves some day without Christ, to find that we had lost him, to look for him in some great need and find that we do not have him anymore?

There is a striking little story by Henry van Dyke, called the Lost Word. It is a story of one of the early centuries. Hermas had become a Christian. He belonged to a wealthy and distinguished pagan family. His father disinherited him and drove him from his home when he accepted the new faith. From being one of the richest young men in Antioch, he was now one of the poorest. In the Grove of Daphne one day he was sitting in sadness by a gushing spring, when there came to him a priest of Apollo, a pagan philosopher, who, seeing his unhappy mood began to talk with him. In the end the old man had made this compact with Hermas. He assured him of wealth, of favor, of success, and Hermas was to give him only a word—but he was to part forever with the name of Him he had learned to worship. "Let me take that word and all that belongs to it entirely out of your life, so that you shall never need to hear it or speak it again. I promise you everything," said the old man, "and this is all I ask in return. Do you consent?" "Yes, I consent," said Hermas. So he lost the word, the Blessed Name.

He has sold it. It was not his anymore. He went back to Antioch, to his old home. There he found his father dying. For hours he had been calling for his son. The old man received him eagerly, said he had forgiven him, and asked his son for his forgiveness. He then asked Hermas to tell him the secret of the Christian faith which he had chose. "You found something that made you willing to give up life for it. What was it you found?" The father was dying and his pagan belief gave him no comfort. He wanted now to know the Christian's secret. Hermas began to tell his father the secret of his faith. "Father," he said, "you must believe with all our heart and soul and strength in –" Where was the word? What was the name? What had become of it? He groped in darkness—but could not find it. There was a lonely soul, crying out for the Name—but Hermas could not tell even his own dying father what it was. The word was lost.

Love came into his life and happiness was heaped on happiness. A child was born to him. But in all the wondrous joy something was lacking. Both he and his wife confessed it. They sought a dismantled shrine in the garden and Hermas sought to pour out his heart. "For all good gifts," he said, "for love, for life, we praise, we bless, we thank –" But he could not find the word. The Name was beyond his reach. There was no one to thank. He had lost God.

The boy grew into wondrous beauty. One day Hermas was victorious in the chariot races. Then he took his boy in the chariot and again drove round the ring to show him to the people. The tumult frightened the horses and they ran away. The child was tossed off and when his father turned to look for him, he was lying like a broken flower on the sand. His distress was great. Days passed. "Is there nothing that we can do?" said the mother. "Is there no one to pity us? Let us pray for his life." Hermas sank on his knees beside his wife. "Out of the depths," he began "– out of the depths, we call for pity. The light of our eyes is fading. Spare the child's life, O merciful –" But there was only a deathly blank. He could not find the Name. The word he wanted was lost.

This story has become true in actual life thousands of times. People have given up the name of Christ, sold it for money, or pleasure, or power, or sin. Then when times of need came, and they turned to find help, there was only blankness. In a home there is some great distress. One is near unto death, and friends want to pray for him. But they cannot pray. In childhood they were taught the words. "Our Father," but long since they have lost the holy Name, and now, when they would give worlds to go to God—they cannot find the way.

In all the world, there is no sadness so deep as the sadness of one who has lost Christ and then in some great need is trying to find him. There is no ear to hear. It is a fearful thing to give up Christ, to lose him. "Without me you can do nothing."

We must not press these words too far. Of course there are certain things men can do who are without Christ, who have no connection with him. There are people who are very useful, benefactors to others, who never pray, who do not love Christ. One may be an artist and paint lovely pictures, pictures which the world will admire, and yet may not believe in Christ, or even think of him. One may be a writer and prepare beautiful books which shall interest others and enlighten, cheer, and inspire many lives to noble deeds—and yet really disregard Christ, be altogether without Christ. One may be a patriot soldier, fighting the battles of freedom or country, or a statesman leading his land to honor—and yet not know Christ, nor be able to get to him. A man may be a good father, kind to his family, making his home beautiful with the loveliest adornments, and rich with refinement and gentleness, providing for his children not only things their bodies need—but providing also for their mental needs and cravings—and know nothing of Christ. There are homes of luxury and refinement, homes of culture, in which there is no prayer, where Christ is never welcomed as a Guest. There may be natural affection, father love, mother love, love of husband and wife, love of friends—yet no love for Christ.

When Jesus says, "Apart from me you can do nothing," we must understand his meaning. He does not say we cannot live good lives, cannot be good merchants, good lawyers, good teachers, good fathers and mothers—but what he means is that we cannot have the joy and blessing of spiritual life—we cannot do the things of God.

The relation between Christ and his friends is closer than any human relation. No one can say to any friend, "Without me you can do nothing." The mother cannot say it to her child. It is a sore loss when the mother of a baby is taken away—but how sore a loss no words can explain. Even God cannot twice give a mother. No other one, however loving and tender in spirit, however gentle in care, however wise in guiding and helping the young life—can be to it all that its own mother could have been. Yet even the best and holiest mother cannot say to her child, "Without me you can do nothing." The child, though so bereft, lives and may live nobly without a mother.

There are other earthly friendships that become so much to those to whom they are given that they seem to be indispensable. The trusting, clinging wife may say to her husband, who is being taken away from her: "I cannot live without you. If you leave me, I will die. I cannot face the cold winds—without your shelter. I cannot go on with the tasks, the cares, the struggles, the responsibilities, the sorrows of life— without your comradeship, your love, your cheer, your strong support, your brave confidence and wise guidance." So it seems to her as she stands amid the wrecks of her hopes. But when he is gone—the strong man on whom she has leaned so confidingly, she takes up the duties of life, its cares, its trying experiences, its tasks, its battles—and goes on for long years with splendid faithfulness and great bravery.

"I never dreamed that I could possibly get along as I have," said a woman after a year of widowhood. Then she told of her utter faintness when she realized that she would no more have her husband's comradeship. She had never had a care or a responsibility unshared by him. As she turned away from his grave it seemed to her that now she was utterly alone. But Christ was with her. Peace came into her heart, calmness came, and then courage began to revive. She grew strong and self reliant. She was a marvel to her friends as she took up her work. She showed resources which none ever dreamed she had. Her sorrow had elevated her. She lived and lived grandly now, without the one who had seemed essential to her very existence.

So we learn that no human life however close it has been is ever actually indispensable to another life. To no one, no human friend, can we say, "I cannot live without you." The taking away of the human, reveals God.

But note what Jesus says, "Apart from me you can do nothing." As the vine is essential to the life of the branch, so is Christ essential to us. We cannot meet any of the serious experiences of life, without Christ. A wonderful change came upon the disciples as they lived with Christ, heard his teaching, let his influence into their lives. They were transformed. They never could have done anything without Christ.

Do without Christ! You do not know what Christ has been to you, even when you were not aware that he was your Friend. You think he has not been doing anything for you, when, in fact, he has been crowning you with loving kindness and tender mercies all your days. If we were to lose Christ today out of our life, as Hermas in the story lost him, if his name were utterly blotted out, his friendship and help taken utterly from our life—what a dark, sad world this would be for us! Think of going out tomorrow to your duty, struggle, danger, responsibility, without Christ, unable to find him in your need. Think of not having Christ in your day of sorrow! Think of dying without Christ!

But we do not have to do without Christ. Only by our own rejection, can we cut ourselves off from him.

Chapter 7

The One Who Stands By

Spirit of God, descend upon my heart;
Wean it from earth; through all its pulses move;
Stoop to my weakness, mighty as You art,
And make me love You as I ought to love.

Teach me to love You, as Your angels love,
One holy passion filling all my frame;
The baptism of the heaven descended Dove,
My heart an altar, and your love the flame.

Jesus spoke to his disciples of the Holy Spirit, as the *Paraclete*. The word used in our translation is *Comforter*. The name is very beautiful and suggestive. We think of a comforter as one who gives consolation in trouble. There is much sorrow in the world, and there is always need of those who understand the art of comforting. Not many do. Job spoke of his friends, who came to offer him consolation in his great trouble, as "miserable comforters." They certainly were. Their words as he heard them, were like thorns. They only *added* to his suffering. There are those in every place who want to be comforters. When they see one in pain or in tears they think they must comfort him. So they begin to say things which they suppose they ought to say. They are sincere enough—but they do not know what they should say. Their words give no strength; they only make the grief seem deeper, sadder, and more hopeless. They are mere empty platitudes; or they misinterpret the sorrows of their friends. That was what Job's "comforters" did.

There is constant need for true comforters. Barnabas is called, a "son of consolation." No doubt he was a sunshiny man. No other one can be a consoler. When Barnabas went into a sick room, we are quite sure his presence was a benediction. When he visited the homes of those who were sorrowing, he carried the light of heaven in his face, and his words were full of uplifting. It is a great thing to be a son or daughter of consolation. Christ himself was a wonderful comforter. The words he spoke were words of eternal truth on which we may lay our heads, and find that we are leaning on the arm of God. No doubt, too, the Holy Spirit is a comforter. He brings the truth of eternal life to those who are bereft. He brings the gentleness and healing of divine love to hurt hearts. The name of Comforter describes well one kind of work the Spirit does in the world.

But the best scholars agree that "comforter" is not the word which most fully and clearly gives the sense of the Greek word which our Lord used. It is Paraclete. The word is used only a few times in the New Testament, and only by John. In the Fourth Gospel it is always translated *Comforter*. Then in John's First Epistle, it is translated *Advocate*. Advocate is perhaps the more accurate translation—not merely a comforter who consoles us in trouble, and makes us stronger to endure sorrow— one who stands by us. The word Advocate is very suggestive. One of its meanings is a person who stands by; strictly, a person called to the side of another. The thought of one who stands by is very suggestive.

It may be said that this is one of the finest definitions of a friend that could be given. He must be one who always stands by you. This does not mean in a human friend that he must always be close to you, always manifesting affection in some practical way, always speaking words of cheer. He may be miles away in space—but you know that he is always loyal to you, true to you, your friend wherever he may be. He always stands by you. He may not be able to do many things for you. Indeed, it is but little that a friend, your best friend, really can do at any time for you. He cannot lift away your load—no other one can bear your burden for you. Each one must bear his own burden. Each one must meet his own life's questions, make his own decisions, endure his own troubles, fight his own battles, and accept his own responsibilities. The office of a friend is not to do things for you, to make life easy for you.

But you know that he always stands by you. You know that if ever you need him in any way and turn to him, that he will not fail you nor disappoint you; that if you do not see him for months, or even for years, nor hear from him, and if you then should go to him with some question or some appeal, you will find him unchanged, the same staunch, strong, faithful friend as always. Though your circumstances have changed, from wealth to poverty, from influence to powerlessness, from popular favor to obscurity, from strength to weakness, still your friend is the same, stands by you as he did before, meets you with the old cordiality, the old kindness, the old helpfulness. Your friend is one who stands by you. That is the kind of friend the Holy Spirit is. You are sure he is always the same, always faithful and true.

Jesus said the Father would give "another Comforter," that is, one like Jesus himself. He was an advocate for his disciples, who always stood by them, their comrade, their defender, and their shelter in danger. His friendship was unchanged through the years. "Loved once" was never said of him. Having loved, he loved unto the end. His disciples failed him, grieved him, disappointed him—but when they came back to him they found him the same, waiting to receive them. Peter denied him in the hour of his deepest need, saying he did not know him; but when Jesus was risen again, the first one of his disciples he asked for was Peter, and when Peter found him, he was still standing by, the same dear, loyal friend.

Jesus said that they would receive another comforter, when he was gone. He wanted them to understand that he was not really going away from them. They would not see his face, would not feel any hands—but he would be there, as he always had been—still standing by. They would lose nothing by his going away. Indeed he would not be gone from them at all. In the Paraclete he would still be with them and would still be their Comforter, their Comrade.

Jesus tells us that the Comforter is more to us—than he himself was to his disciples. He said that it was expedient for them that he should go away, for then the Comforter would come. Think what it was to have their Master for a personal friend. There never was such another Friend. Think of his gentleness, his tenderness, his sympathy, his kindness, the inspiration of his life. Think of the shelter he was to them, the strength, and the encouragement. Then remember what he said the Holy Spirit would be—"another Comforter," one like Christ, and that it would be more to us to have the Holy Spirit for our friend than if Jesus had stayed with us. He is everything to us that Jesus was to his personal friends. He is our Advocate. He always stands by us, and for us. His love is unchanging.

We talk of the love of the *Father*. We are his children. He loves us. He comforts us with his wonderful tenderness. We talk and sing of the love of *Christ* as the most marvelous revelation of love the world ever saw. But we do not speak or sing so much of the love of the *Spirit*. Yet the Spirit's love is just as wonderful as the Father's or the Son's. For one thing, he loves us enough to come and live in our hearts. Does that seem a little thing? We speak a great deal, especially at Christmas time, of the condescension of the eternal Son of God in coming to earth, to be born in a stable and cradled in a manger. Is it a less wonderful condescension for the Holy Spirit to make your heart his home, to be borne there, to live there as your Guest? Think what a place a human heart is. The stable where Jesus was born was lowly—but it was clean. Are our hearts clean? Think of the unholy thoughts, the unholy desires, the impure things, the unlovingness, the jealousy, the bitterness, the hate, all the sin of our hearts. Then think of the love of the Spirit that makes him willing to live in such a foul place, in order to cleanse us and make us upright and holy.

The love of the Spirit is shown in his wondrous patience with us in all our sinfulness, while he lives in us and deals with us in the culturing of our Christian life. We speak often of the patient love of Christ with his disciples the three years he was with them, having them in his family, at his table, enduring their ignorance, their dullness, their narrowness, their petty strifes, and their unfaithfulness. It was a marvelous love that never grew weary of them—which loved on in spite of all that so tried his love, which endured the hate of men, their plotting, their treacheries, and their cruelty. We never can understand the depth of the love of Christ in enduring all that he endured in saving the world. But think also of the love of the Holy Spirit in what he suffers in his work with us. Paul beseeches us that we grieve not the Holy Spirit. The word "grieve" in the original is from the same root as the word used in the Gospel when we are told that the soul of Jesus in the Garden was *exceeding sorrowful*. Think of that. We make a *Gethsemane* in our heart for the Holy Spirit every time we doubt him; or grieve him by our thoughts, our disobedience.

A young Christian woman relates an experience which greatly saddened her. She had a girl friend that she had long loved deeply. The two were inseparable. They trusted each other implicitly. One who tells the story says she had regarded her friend as like an angel in the truth and beauty of her life. She never had had a shadow of doubt concerning her character and conduct. Then she learned that this girl had been living a double life for years. The discovery appalled her. At first she refused to believe it—but the evidence was so clear, so unmistakable, that she could not but believe it, and it almost killed her. It was painful to hear her words and see her distress. Then she wrote: "I understand now a little of the bitter sorrow of my Savior in Gethsemane, as he drank the cup of his people's sins."

If a human friend can be thus brokenhearted over the sin of a friend, how the Holy Spirit must suffer in his nourishing of us, in his watching for our sanctification, in his wondrous brooding over us—but how he must grieve when we fall into sin!

Chapter 8

Love's Best at Home

In the home, love should come to its best. There it should reach its richest beauty. The song it sings there, should be its sweetest. All love's marvelous possibilities should be realized in the life of the home. Whatever love may achieve in any other relation or condition, home is the place where its lessons should be most perfectly learned. Home ought to be the holiest place on earth. It is to be a place of confidence. We are to trust each other perfectly there. There is never to be a shadow of doubt, suspicion, or lack of confidence in the home fellowships. There should need to be no locked doors, no hidden secrets, no disloyalties, no enmities, and no diverse interests, in the home relations. We should understand each other there. We should live together in perfect frankness and confidence. Each should honor the other. We should see good and never evil, in the others. We should trust each other. Our life together in the home should be characterized by perfect truth. Familiarity should never make us treat one another in any way which would give offence. The most familiar intimacy should not permit us ever to disregard the proprieties and amenities of the truest refinement. We should be more courteous in our homes, than anywhere else in the world.

All the Christian virtues should find their exemplification in the home life. "Love suffers long, and is kind." That is, love never wearies in suffering whether it be in its service of others or in the enduring of unkindness at the hands of others. Love continually demands self-denial and sacrifice, for the sake of others. When we say to another in whatever relation, "I am going to be your friend," we do not begin to know what it is going to mean to us to keep our word. We have to be always denying ourselves, giving up our own way, sacrificing our rights, giving our friend the pleasures we had expected to enjoy ourselves.

The story of friendship anywhere, is a story of cost and suffering—but it is in the home that it must suffer the most, make the greatest sacrifices. When husband and wife clasp hands at the marriage altar, they can fulfill their covenant of love only by mutual loving unto death. It may cost either of them a great deal to love as they have promised to do, until death separates them. Here is a man who loves his wife with a devoted affection. For ten years she has been a helpless invalid, and he has carried her from the bed to the chair, and up and down stairs, and has ministered to her in a most beautiful way, failing in nothing that she needed or craved, pouring out his life's best treasures to give her comfort or pleasure. This is ideal. So it should be in all the home relations. Love that stops at no cost, at no sacrifice, should be the law of the home life.

It should be the same with all the qualities of love. We are to exercise patience with every person we may meet, in all the relations of life—but we should show the sweetest and most Christlike patience in our own homes. Kindness is the great law of Christian life. It should be the universal law. We should be kind to everyone, not only to those who treat us with love—but also to those who are ungentle to us, returning to them love for hate. But in our own home and toward our own, our kindness should not only be unvarying—but be always exceptionally tender.

A writer suggests that members of a family, when they separate for the night or even for the briefest stay, should never part in any way but an affectionate way, lest they shall never meet again. Two incidents illustrate the importance of this rule. A distinguished man, when much past middle life, related an experience which occurred in his own home in his young manhood. At the breakfast table one morning he and a younger brother had a sharp quarrel about some unimportant matter. He confessed that he was most unbrotherly in his words, speaking with bitterness. The brother rose and left the table and went to his business, very angry. Before noon the younger man died suddenly in his office. When, twenty years afterward, the older brother spoke of the occurrence, he said that it had cast a shadow over all his life. He could never forgive himself for his part in the bitter quarrel. He had never ceased to regret with sore pain that no opportunity had come to him to confess his fault and seek forgiveness and reconciliation.

The other incident was of the parting of a working man and his wife. He was going forth to his day's duties and there was a peculiar tenderness in his mood and in their good bye that morning. He and his wife had their prayer together after breakfast. Then he kissed the babies, sleeping in their cribs, and returned a second time to look into their sweet faces. The parting at the door never had been so tender as it was that morning. Before half the day was gone, he was brought home dead. The wife got great comfort in her sorrow from the memory of the morning's parting. If their last words together had been marked by unkindness, by wrangling or quarreling, or even by indifference, or lack of tenderness, her grief would have been harder to bear. But the lovingness of the last parting took away much of the bitterness of the sorrow.

If we keep ourselves ever mindful of the *fragility* of life, that any day may be the last in our home fellowships, it will do much to make us gentle and kind to each other. We will not act selfishly any hour, for it may be our last hour together. We will not let strife mar the good cheer of our home-life any day, for we may not have another day.

Not much is told of our Lord's home life—but the few glimpses we have of it assure us that it was wondrously loving. Jesus was sinless, and we are sure, therefore, that nothing he ever said or did caused the slightest bitterness in any home heart. He never lost his temper, never grew angry, never showed any impatience, never was stubborn or willful, never was selfish, and never did anything thoughtless, never failed in kindness. We have enough hints of his gracious love for his mother down to his last kindly thought of her on his cross, to make us sure that he continued to the close, to be to her the perfect son.

It will help us in learning our lesson in its details if we will look at some Scripture words about love and apply them to the life of the home. "Love suffers long, and is kind." There come experiences in the life of many homes in which one has to suffer, make sacrifices, endure pain or loss, and bear burdens almost without measure, for the sake of the others. This is Christlike, though costly. "She is wasting her life," said one, indignantly, of the eldest daughter of a family. "She is denying herself all leisure, all good times, staying at home, working for the other children and her little mother, while they go out into society and have their pleasures. She is pouring out her life to give them the privileges they crave." Yes—but always some must toil while others rest; some must bear burdens while others go tripping along without question or care; some must sacrifice to the uttermost, while others indulge themselves. It may seem unfair, unjust—yet that is love, and it is by love that the world lives. The oil is consumed in the lamp—but the room glows with light. One life is consumed in service, misses the world's pleasures, goes without rest—but the home is made joyous and all things go smoothly. It scarcely seems fair to the one who sacrifices so—but that is love, and love is the greatest force for good and blessing in the world.

There is more of the picture. There are few more hateful things in the world than envy, and in no other place is envy so hateful as when it appears in the home. Love drives out envy. "Love does not boast, is not puffed up." Love is humble, lowly, does not strut, does not assert itself, and does not assume superiority. There are homes in which there is too much pompous vaunting, where one lords it over others. But it is most unbeautiful, most utterly unloving.

"Love does not behave unseemly." Anything that is crude, ungentle, unrefined, discourteous, is unseemly, unfit. So love takes note of coarseness in behavior, of bad manners. "I am not required to mind everybody's tender points," one may say. "I cannot be ruled by other people's sensitiveness." Yet one who loves as Jesus loved—is considerate of others even if others are over sensitive. That is what thoughtfulness teaches. Boorishness in others never makes it right for us to be boorish in return. It is in the home that this refinement is most beautiful and does most for making happiness. The love that is most divine, does not behave itself unseemly. Godly people may be awkward, may not understand the rules of etiquette, may unconsciously violate the dictates of fashion at table or in society, and yet not behave unseemly. What is required is the gentle spirit in the heart that would not give pain to anyone, though it may know nothing of the arbitrary rules of fashion. For one may never fail in the smallest things of society manners, and yet in heart may be most unrefined and unseemly.

The lesson runs on. "Love seeks not its own." This is the heart of the whole matter. *Seeking its own* is the *poison* of all life. Love never seeks its own—but it always thinks of the other person. If this were the universal rule in our homes there would be no disputes, no strifes, no asserting of ourselves; each would serve the other. "Love is not easily provoked." Getting provoked is the danger always in every place where lives meet and mingle. Many people are touchy and fly into anger at the slightest provocation. This is the bane of too much home life—it is hurt ofttimes by impatience and irritability. It is given to quick retorts. It resents suggestion and question. It does not restrain itself nor check its bitter feeling. It is given to hasty speech. The love that is not provoked gives only gentle replies, however crude and irritating the words spoken may be. Such loving, with its soft answers which turn away wrath, is a prime secret of home happiness.

These are only a few of the specific qualities of love which are mentioned in a few verses of one chapter of the New Testament. Many more might be cited. These rules of love were not given specifically with reference to home life—but as to the way a Christian should live anywhere. They are suggested here as touching the home, because home is where love should always reach its best. Home should be *love's school*; there we should learn *love's lessons*. Then when we go out into the world and take up our tasks and duties—we will be ready for them, and the lessons we have learned in the *school of home* we shall go on practicing in daily life.

Is it not time we tried to make more of our homes? It is not time we got more love into them? For one thing, there is pitiful need of cheer and encouragement in most homes. There is more *blame* heard than *praise*. There are those who give their lives without reserve for the good of the household, and scarcely ever hear a word of thanks. How much comfort and help it would give, to hear now and then a word of appreciation! How it would cheer many a wife and mother whose life is given out in untiring work, if she heard words of praise from those for whom she lives! It is not *monuments when they are dead* that women want—but they would rather a thousand times have a simple word of kindness and appreciation, day by day, as they toil.

Says Hugh Black: "In our relation with each other, there is usually more advantage to be reaped from friendly *encouragement*, than from friendly *correction*. There are more lives spoiled by undue *harshness*, than by undue *gentleness*. More good work is lost from lack of appreciation than from too much of it; and certainly it is not the function of friendship to do the critic's work."

No crowns in heaven will be brighter than those shall wear who have lived out love's lessons in their own homes. Nearly everyone has known some home, in which nearly all of whose light has come from one member of the household. Frederick W. Robertson, referring to such a life, asks: "What was the secret of her power? What had she done? Absolutely nothing; but radiant smiles, beaming good humor, the tact of knowing what everyone wanted, told that she had got out of *self* and had learned to think of others; so that at one time it showed itself in deprecating the quarrel, which lowers brows and raised tones already showed to be impending, by sweet words; at another by smoothing an invalid's pillow; at another by soothing a sobbing child; at another by humoring and softening a father who had returned weary and ill tempered from the irritating cares of business. None but she saw those things."

Chapter 9

What About Bad Temper?

What about bad temper? An English writer said that more than half of us are bad tempered. He gave the figures. He arranged to have about two thousand people put unconsciously under espionage as to their ordinary temper, and then had careful reports of the results tabulated. The footing up is decidedly unflattering to the two thousand people who were thus treated. More than half of them—to be entirely accurate, fifty two percent of them—are set down as bad tempered in various degrees. The dictionary has been well near exhausted in giving the different shades of badness. Acrimonious, aggressive, bickering, captious, choleric, contentious, crotchety, despotic, domineering, easily offended, gloomy, grumpy, harsh, huffy, irritable, morose, obstinate, peevish, sulky, surly, vindictive—these are some of the qualifying words. There are employed, in all, forty six terms, none of which describes a sweet temper.

We do not like to believe that the case is so serious—but most of us are unnamiable and offensive, in some degree. It is much easier to confess our neighbor's faults and infirmities, than our own; so, therefore, quietly taking refuge for ourselves among the forty eight percent of good natured people, we shall probably be willing to admit that a great many of the people we know have at times rather uncommendable tempers. They are easily provoked. They fly into a passion on every slight occasion. They are haughty, domineering, peevish, fretful, or resentful.

What is even worse, most of them appear to make no *effort* to grow out of their infirmities of disposition. The unripe fruit does not come to mellowness in the passing years. The roughness is not polished off to reveal the diamond's lustrous beauty. The same impetuous pride, vanity, selfishness, and other disagreeable qualities remain in the life year after year. The person does not seem to grow any *sweeter*. When there is a struggle to overcome one's faults and grow out of them, and where the progress toward better and more beautiful spiritual character year after year is perceptible, though the progress is ever so slow—we should have patience. But where one appears unconscious of one's blemishes, and makes no effort to conquer one's failings, there is little ground for encouragement. Hope starts in a life when one begins to try to overcome the evil, to cast out the wrong, to strive for the likeness of Christ.

When a man thinks he is perfect, he is not only pitifully imperfect—but he is in a condition in which no one can do anything to help him. He is unconscious of any lack, and his lack is hopeless. But when a man begins to realize that he is weak and faulty and incomplete, he is ready to begin to grow out of his faults and is at the beginning of a struggle which will end in the victory over himself and growth into completeness of character.

Bad temper is such a disfigurement of character, and besides works such harm to oneself and one's neighbors, that no one should spare any pains or cost to have it cured. The ideal Christian life is one of unbroken kindliness. It is dominated by love, the love whose portrait is so exquisitely drawn for us in the immortal thirteenth chapter of First Corinthians. "Love is patient, love is kind. It does not envy, it does not boast, it is not proud. It is not rude, it is not self-seeking, it is not easily angered, it keeps no record of wrongs. Love does not delight in evil but rejoices with the truth. It always protects, always trusts, always hopes, always perseveres. Love never fails." That is the picture.

Then we have but to turn to the Gospel pages to find the story of a Life in which all these beautiful things were realized. Jesus never lost his temper. He lived among people who tried him at every point, some by their dullness, and others by their bitter enmity and persecution—but he never failed in sweetness, in patience, in self-denying love. Like those flowers that give out their perfume only when *crushed*, like the odoriferous wood which bathes with fragrance the axe that *hews* it—the life of Christ yielded only the sweetest love to the rough impact of men's rudeness and wrong. That is the pattern on which we should strive to fashion our life and character. Every outbreak of violent temper, every shade of ugliness in disposition, mars the radiant loveliness of the picture we are seeking to have fashioned in our souls. Whatever is not lovely—is unlovely.

There is another phase; bad tempered people are continually hurting others, ofttimes their best friends. Some people are sulky, and one person's sulkiness casts a shadow over the whole household. Other people are over sensitive, ever watching for slights and offended by the merest trifles, so that even their closest friends have to be always on the watch, lest they offend them. Others are despotic and will brook no kindly suggestion nor listen to any expression of opinion. Others are so quarrelsome that even the meekest and gentlest person cannot live peaceably with them. Whatever may be the special characteristic of a bad temper, it makes only pain and humiliation for the person's friends.

Usually, *bad temper* is accompanied by a *sharp tongue*. A brother and sister are said often to have passed months without speaking to each other, though eating at the same table and sleeping under the same roof. There recently died a man who, for twelve years, it was currently said, had never spoken to his wife, nor had she to him, although three times every day they sat at the same table. She would serve him with his coffee and he would serve her with the meat—but their glumness never relaxed into a word of courtesy. Bad temper sometimes runs to unyielding silence. Such silence is not of the kind the proverb calls golden. Usually, however, a bad tempered person finds a tongue and speaks out the hateful feelings of his heart. There is no limit to the pain and the harm which their words produce in gentle hearts.

Is there no cure for this? Must a bad tempered person always remain bad tempered? Or is there a way by which the evil may be transformed? No doubt the grace of God is able to make the old, new. There is no temper so obdurately bad, that it cannot be trained into sweetness. The grace of God can take the most unlovely life—and make it into the image of Christ. As in all moral changes, however, grace does not work independently of human volition and exertion. God always works helpfully with those who strive to reach Christ-likeness. We must struggle to obtain the victory over our own evil disposition and habits, although it is only through Christ that we can fully succeed. He will not make us conquerors, unless we enter the battle. We have a large and necessary share in the culture of our own character. The bad tempered man will never become good tempered, until he deliberately sets for himself the task and enters resolutely and persistently upon its accomplishment. The transformation will never come of itself, even in a Christian. People do not grow out of an ugly temper into sweet refinement, as a peach ripens from sourness into lusciousness.

What is it exactly that is to be accomplished? It is not the destruction of the temper. Temper is good in its place. The task to be achieved is to win self-control. The truly strong man is he who is strong in temper, that is, which has strong passions and feelings, capable of great anger, and then has perfect self mastery. The task to be set, therefore, in self discipline, is the gaining of mastery over every feeling, and emotion, so as to be able to restrain every impulse, and never to act unadvisedly. "The best characters are made by vigorous and persistent resistance to evil tendencies; whose amiability has been built upon the ruins of ill temper, and whose generosity springs from an overmastered and transformed selfishness. Such a character, built up in the presence of enemies, has far more attraction than one which is natively pleasing."

Then there is need of a higher standard of attainment in this regard, than many people seem to set for themselves. *We never rise higher than our ideals.* The perfect beauty of Christ should always be visioned in our hearts, as that which we would attain for ourselves. The honor of our Master's name should impel us to strive ever toward Christ likeness in spirit and disposition. We represent our Master in this world. People cannot see *him*, and they must look at *us* to see in our lives a little at least of what he is like. Whatever great work we may do for Christ, if we fail to live out his life of patience and forbearance, we fail in an essential part of our duty as Christians. "The Lord's servant must be *gentle*."

We never can be greatly useful in the world while our daily conduct is marred by frequent outbursts of anger and other exhibitions of temper. Only as our own lives shine in the brightness of holy affectionateness, and our hearts and lips distill the sweetness of patience and gentleness, can we fulfill our mission in this world as Christ's true messengers to men. The thing in others which irritates us is ofttimes balanced by something in us which looks just as unlovely in their eyes, and which just as sorely tries their forbearance toward us.

If we think our neighbors are hard to live with—they probably think the same of us; then who shall tell in whom lies the greater degree of fault? It is certain at least that a really good natured person can rarely ever be drawn into a quarrel with anyone. He is resolutely determined that he will not be a partner in any unseemly strife. He would rather suffer wrongfully, than offer any retaliation. He has learned to bear and to forbear. Then, by his gentle tact—he is able to conciliate those who are angry.

The *fault* must never be ours, if there is a difference or a quarrel which we cannot ward off. "As much as in us lies," Paul tells us, "we should be at peace with all men." A wise man says, "Every man takes care that his neighbors shall not cheat him—but a day comes when he begins to take care that he does not cheat his neighbors." So long as a man sees only the quarrelsome temper of his neighbor, he is not far toward saintliness; but when he has learned to watch and to try to control his own temper, and to weep over his own infirmities—he is on the way to God, and will soon conquer his own weakness. We find in the end—that it is *ourselves* which needs watching.

Life is too short for us to spend even one day or one hour of it, in bickering and strife. Love is too sacred to be lacerated and torn by the ugly briers of sharp temper! Surely we ought to learn to be patient with others, since God has to show every day—such infinite patience toward us. Is not the very essence of true love, the spirit that is not easily provoked, that bears all things? Can we not, then, train our lives to sweeter gentleness? Can we not learn to be touched even a little roughly without resenting it and growing angry? Can we not bear little injuries and apparent injustices, without flying into an unfitting rage? Can we not have in us, something of the mind of Christ which will enable us, like him, to endure all wrong and injury—and give back no word or look of bitterness? The way over which we and our friend walk together—is too short to be spent in *wrangling*.

Chapter 10

The Engagement Ring

No hour in all a woman's life means more to her—than the hour when she knows that she is loved, and that she loves. Her heart has found its home. She has been chosen from among all women in the world by a noble and worthy man—to be the queen of his life. Her heart responds to the affection which has poured itself upon her. She is very happy. Her happiness makes her face radiant.

This hour ought to be with her a time of deep *thoughtfulness*. It should be a time of *fearlessness*. Perfect love casts out fear. No girl is ready to announce her engagement, if she is anxious and afraid in any degree concerning the matter. She must have perfect trust in the man to whom she has pledged her love. If she has not, she should wait longer until she is sure.

In her thought of what she is about to do, she must think much on the question, whether the man who asks her hand will meet all the needs of her nature. It is not enough that he is able to provide a *home of comfort* for her to live in. This is not all that is requisite for her happiness. She may have a palace of luxury and may not lack anything that money can provide—and yet be miserable.

It is not enough, either, that he is a man of *ability* and *rank*. He may stand high among men and may appear to be in every way noble and worthy. He may be gifted, talented, and brilliant. He may seem to have in him all the essential qualities of manliness. He may be brave and strong and true. Women are attracted by *greatness*. They worship the *heroic*. They admire men who can do great things. Weakness and timidity they dislike. They are not won by cowardice and inefficiency. The man who is bold, fearless, who is not intimidated by danger, whom no difficulty can daunt and no obstacle can defeat, appeals to them irresistibly.

But *strength* is not all a woman needs in the man to whom she would commit herself for the keeping and cherishing which a husband promises in the marriage contract. He may be brave and powerful, and yet may lack *tenderness*. Strength and tenderness are united in the ideal life—but *strength without gentleness will make no woman happy.* She craves love. Her heart needs tenderness. There will come days in her life when her heart is hungry, when she is in sorrow, when she is suffering, and when even the noblest strength will not be to her, all that she craves. The most brilliant natural gifts will not then satisfy her. She wants then to be loved. She must have the gentle word, the kindly sympathy, the soothing touch. Courage is a fine quality—but courage may be *brutal*. It may be crude, tyrannical, and pitiless. True, manly courage—is as gentle as a mother with her child.

Jan Carlyle said, "I married for *ambition*; and my husband has exceeded all that my wildest hopes ever imagined of him—but I am miserable!" She married a genius, and got a husband who broke her heart by his churlish tyranny. The world praised him, and wrote his name high up on fame's column; but what comfort was that, to the gentle woman who was crushed by his miserable ungentleness, and never heard a kindly word from his lips? The ideal man is brave. He is true. He is strong. He is upright. But if a man is brave and true and strong and upright—and yet is crude, unfeeling, and ungentle—he is not going to be a comfort to his wife through the varying experiences of her life. There will come days when amid all the luxury and splendor her husband will provide, her heart will cry out for *simple tenderness*. There will be hours when she would give all the wealth, the honor, the brilliant name, the world's adulation, which her husband brings to her—for something of the *sweetness of common kindness*. The girl should think of this when she is planning for her marriage.

She must ask another question—whether she is able to fulfill *her part* in the marriage compact into which she is about to enter. Can she meet the needs of the man who asks her to be his wife? Can she inspire in him the latent qualities of nobleness and power which wait for the touch of a woman's hand? Can she do her part in making him the man he *ought* to be, the man he *may* be? It will not be enough that she has the expectation of fine social position, of a brilliant marriage. If she has in her mind the true thought of the matter, that which will press most heavily upon her heart will be what she is going to make of herself, the woman she is going to be. She is loved, and love should wake up in her all the slumbering powers of her being.

In one of the Psalms there is a suggestive prayer: "Awake, my glory. Awake, psaltery and harp. I myself will awake right early." There is a glory in everyone of us, some power of nobleness, some hidden beauty, some possible worth, some seed which may grow into a heavenly plant, and some bud which may open into a wondrous flower. The commonest life has glory in it—but it may yet be sleeping. It is a holy moment when we become even dimly conscious that we have any measure of glory in us, and begin really to pray that it may be awakened. It is a blessed hour when a young person for the first time prays, "Awake, my glory," and then declares, "I myself will awake right early." In too many, the call to awake is never heard and the glory sleeps on.

Love is an experience which, if allowed to work itself out freely, calls for the awakening of the best that is in the life. It stirs the whole being. The prayer in the old Psalm reveals the consciousness of music slumbering in the soul, and calls for its awakening. "Awake, psaltery and harp." There are strings with marvelous capacity for music which have never given out a note. The poet calls upon these to awake. There is music in our lives which is sleeping, and never has been awakened. Love should awaken every sleeping chord. When love has come into a girl's heart, she should become aware of a thousand possibilities of beauty, of sweetness, of noble character in herself. She is not yet the girl she *may* become, and *ought* to become. Love is waking her up, and she begins to feel a thousand longings for the lovely things she sees in her vision. The revealings she has, are glimpses of what she may be, of what God wants her to be, and she should strive at once to reach them.

Life thus grows serious to the girl to whom love has come. She must set herself the task of becoming *the woman God wants her to be*. Love is calling for her best. Life is trivial and unworthy, if it calls her only to an empty happiness such as sometimes young people think of as life's best. If she is worthy, and if she has any true conception of the finest possibilities of life, the vision which love wakes in her soul is of the blossoming out of all the richest things until they have reached their best and highest. One writes, "The only conceivable thing that can be named as the object of life is character; for the simple reason that it is the only thing which lasts—but to take this self, made up of heart and mind and will, and train it in the line of its creative design, bring out all its powers, train it away from its faults and defects, make it strong and compact and substantial—but a real thing, harmonious, true, the very thing that it was designed to be." Nothing less than this should be the aim of the girl who is dreaming of her marriage.

This is the call of the deepest heart of every true man to the woman he has chosen to be his wife. This is the vision that rises in his soul when he thinks of her. No less radiant and lovely should the vision in her own soul be, as she thinks of the woman she would be when her marriage day comes.

The girl who has accepted love, and announced her engagement, should consecrate her life anew to Christ and commit herself to him in a very special and sacred way. She has always needed Christ. She has needed his protection. Through the days of her childhood and young girlhood, her life has been like a sweet flower exposed to danger and harm of every kind, in peril of being spoiled and crushed, and only the shelter of the strength of Christ has kept her. The warmth of his love has been the summer of her life. The shadow of his might, has been her defense. All that she is and has become she owes to his gentle care through the years of her childhood and youth. But she never needed Christ before, as she needs him now. Life is growing more and more serious to her. New questions are coming to be answered. New responsibilities are arising before her. She is preparing for marriage, and marriage will bring her into new relationships where great wisdom will be required, where mistakes will be perilous, and where only God can do for her, what she needs.

Marriage is thought of by most people entering it as something very beautiful and very happy. It is thought of as a *dream of delight*—but ofttimes as too much of a *dream*, with not enough *reality*. Very soon the two who have begun their wedded life with this *dream vision* in their minds, find that after all marriage is something very serious. No matter how sweet the happiness, how exalted and ethereal the experiences, they cannot live in the skies—but must come down to common earth— the *man* to business, tasks, wages, regular hours, unreasonable people, complications, competitions; the *woman* to housekeeping, meals, domestic cares and frets, questions of income and expense, clothes, neighbors, society, and a thousand things which may be so tactfully met as to make the daily life a beautiful song—or may be so untactfully experienced as to result in the worst kind of discordance.

Wedded life has in it *splendid possibilities of happiness*—the dream continuing amid all the confusing realities of mundane affairs—but it has in it also distressing possibilities of wrangling, disputing, frets, tears, unhappiness, and all manner of bitterness. Those who marry need large measures of patience, good nature, gentleness, and self-control. It requires only a few minutes to go through a ceremony and to be pronounced married—but it takes a good while to be really married—married through and through, so that two lives actually blend in one.

The lesson of self *forgetfulness* has to be learned—love that wearies not, that is not provoked, that thinks no evil, that suffers long and is kind that never fails. Almost never do young people enter the wedded life with no further discipline necessary to prepare them for living together in complete happiness. The time never comes when patience, self restraint, and love in its spirit of mercy, humility, and endurance—are no longer required in living together in unbroken peace. Happiness in marriage is not the result of a ceremony, the putting on of a ring, a honeymoon tour, a beautiful home, and a circle of delightful friends; it is a *lesson* which must be *learned* in joy and in sorrow, a lesson which only Christ can teach.

All this the girl who is planning to marry needs to think of, in the days before the wedding day. She sorely needs Christ in those days. He alone can give her the love which will make her ready to do her part. If she is wise and thoughtful, therefore, she will take Christ into her life, into every phase of it, and will learn to live so sweetly that when she enters the experience of marriage, there will be no fear that it will fail of happiness.

These are only a few suggestions that looking at the engagement ring on the hand of a happy girl, start in the mind. Of course an *engagement ring* is not the only preparation a girl needs to ensure a joyous wedded life; it is not a charm with magical power; she needs a preparation of mind and heart. She needs a self discipline which will bring all the powers of her being into harmony and under a self-control which will make her safe from all impatience, whatever the experience may be. She needs an assimilation of her life and character to Christ's—so that in her soul the image of Christ shall shine. She needs a *trust* in Christ which will lead her to him for strength in every time of need or of danger. She needs a *consecration* to Christ which will keep her faithful to him in all her life. If she thus consciously belongs to Christ—she will take him into her home as her abiding Guest; and where Christ lives—love will live.

Chapter 11

What Christ's Friendship Means

When then Master first looked upon Simon, he saw him as he was, and saw him through and through. When a stranger comes into our presence, we see only his outward appearance. We cannot look into his *heart* nor read the inner secrets of his life. But the look of Jesus that day penetrated to the very depths of Simon's being. He read his character. He saw all his life, what had been good, and what had been evil. "You are Simon," he said.

But that was not all. Jesus not only saw Simon as he was—but he saw also the possibilities that were in him, all that he might become, and this was something very great and very noble. "You are Simon—but you shall be called Cephas." Now he was only a rough fisherman, crude, unrefined, and uneducated, without ability, without power or influence, full of faults. None of the neighbors of Simon saw in him any promise of greatness. They never dreamed of him as attaining the greatness and splendor of character that ultimately he reached. But that day when Simon was introduced to him, Jesus saw all that the old fisherman might become in the years before him.

In a gallery in Europe there stands, side by side, Rembrandt's first picture, a simple sketch, imperfect and faulty, and his great masterpiece, which all men admire. So, in the two names, Simon and Peter, we have two pictures—first, the crude fisherman who came to Jesus that day, the man as he was before Jesus touched his life and began his work on him; and, second, the man as he became during the years when the friendship of Jesus had warmed his heart and enriched his life; when the teaching of Jesus had given him wisdom and started holy aspirations in his soul; and when the experiences of struggle and failure, of penitence and forgiveness, of sorrow and joy, had wrought their transformations in him.

When Jesus said, "You shall be called Cephas," he did not mean that this transformation of Simon would take place instantaneously. The fisherman did not at once become the Rock-man. This was the man into whom he would grow along the years under Christ's tuition and training. This was what his character would be when the work of grace in him should be finished. The new name was a prophecy of the man that was to be, the man Jesus would make of him. Now he was only Simon—rash, impulsive, self confident, vain, and therefore weak and unstable. "You shall be Peter—a stone." That very moment the struggle began in Peter's soul. He had a glimpse of what the Master meant in the new name he gave him, and began to strive toward it.

Think what Jesus was to Peter during the years that followed. He was his teacher, his friend, his inspiration. If Simon had not come to him and entered his school, he would never have been anything but a rough, swearing fisherman, casting his nets for a few years into the Sea of Galilee, then dying unhonored and being buried in an unmarked grave by the sea. His name never would have been known in the world. Think what Peter became, then of what he is today, in history, in influence upon the countless millions of lives that have been blessed through him—all this, because Jesus found him and became his friend.

A new human **friendship** coming into a life, may color all its future and change its destiny. Every contact of life leaves a touch on the character. Think what helpfulness there is in a rich human friendship. It is interesting to follow the stories of friendships as we see them in those we know. Ofttimes it seems as if the friends had met by chance. They were not brought together by any of the processes of association. Nobody planned to have them meet. They did not choose each other and intentionally bring about the beginning of the friendship which meant so much to both of them in the end. Their lives touched—God brought them together—and the touch proved a divine coincidence. One became a potent influence in the formation of the character of the other. When we meet another as if by chance and friendship begins, we never know what it will lead to, what the influence of the companionship will be. It is God who guides such chances and the friendship is brought about by him.

One wrote to another, "Life has been so different to me since you became my friend." It had been easier, for the person had needed guidance, and the hand of the older friend had given steadiness to the life of the younger one. The friendship had brought new inspiration, for the guidance was safe and wise from long experience. The friendship in this case has also brought companionship. Many of us have friendships which came into our lives and have been benedictions, inspirations, a comfort, a strength through all the years that have followed.

We may think of what the friendship of Jesus was to Simon. It set before him a vision of purity, of beauty, of heavenliness, of strength, which gave him new thoughts of life. Nobody he had ever known had had such a life as he saw in Jesus. He had never seen such gentleness before, such graciousness, such patience, such kindness. It was not the supernatural Jesus, the miraculous in power which impressed Simon—but it was the genuineness of his humanity, the simple goodness, the richness of his nature, which first so influenced him. He never had heard such words in his home or among the best people he had known—as the words he now heard Jesus speak.

A young girl, away at school, had a letter from her pastor, and wrote of it, "I never received such a letter as that before." It was entirely different from the letters the young people had written to her, yet it was not a solemn letter, it was not filled with pious platitudes, giving advice, and warning her against danger. She had expected that her pastor's first letter to her would be a serious one, and she almost dreaded receiving it. But instead, every word of it was bright and human, full of cheer, not trivial—but full of inspiration. She never had read such a letter. Yet that letter set her feet in new paths. She was a better girl than ever after receiving it. Life meant more to her from that day. In some such was the friendship of Jesus affected Simon. Jesus was not a bit like the rabbis, the priests, and the rulers to whom the fisherman had been accustomed. He had never heard that kind of religious conversation, nor found that sort of friend until now.

There are some friendships which really make all things new for those into whose lives they come. Life has a new meaning after that. It looks up and sees the blue skies and the stars, where before it saw only dust and barren fields. There is something else to seek for now, besides the day's bread and poor houses to live in. There is something in our friend that makes it easier for us to work, that makes our burdens seem lighter. The griefs that were so hard for us to endure, mean now to us far less of loneliness and bitterness since we have these new friendships.

These are hints only of what the personal friendship of Jesus meant to Simon. Think what uplift there was in the new name the Master gave him. He was going to be a Rock. He certainly was not that now—but just as certainly he would be. "You shall be Peter." In just this same way Jesus comes to us with a new name. We shall not always be poor fishermen—but some day we shall be catching men, some day we shall be great apostles. The life before us is glorious. Jesus sees us first as we are, with all our imperfections, our blemishes, and faults. But he sees also the *possibilities* that are in us. We do not consider enough what we are to be—when the new life in us grows into all its splendor of character. We ought to think of the splendor into which we shall come through Christ's grace. We are not worms; we are immortal beings. We are children of God. We are heirs of heaven. Now we are imperfect and very faulty—but we are going to grow out of all that and become glorious creatures. It is when we realize this and the glorious vision bursts upon us, that we begin to live truly.

The Master sets before us the goal of our being. He has a beautiful plan for each life. There is something definite for which he has made us, into which he would fashion us, and toward which all his guidance, education, and training will tend. *This is not a world of chance—but it is our Father's world.* All the experiences of our lives have their part in making us what Christ would have us become, in bringing out the possibilities that he sees in us when we first come to him.

All life is a school. Our school books are not all in English print. Our lessons are set for us in many kinds of type, in different languages. The Bible is our great text book, and we are to use it daily and always. The lessons are not written out plainly for us on its pages. But *life* is our practice school. There we are to learn patience, joy, contentment, peace, gentleness. All the experiences of the passing days have their lessons in them. Sometimes we are alarmed by the disappointments, the sufferings, the sorrows—which we have to endure. But there really is no reason for alarm or dismay, however full of pain or seeming loss the days may be. God is in his world, and whatever the experiences may be, nothing is going wrong. The disappointments which seem to be working confusion in our hopes and plans—are God's appointments, yielding better things in the end than if our pleasant dreams had been realized. The sufferings and the sorrows of our lives have their part in the working out of the Master's vision for us. Peter owed a great deal to the *hard things* in his education. He paid a large price for his lessons—but not too large.

It is worth while to endure all the sorrow, loss, and pain, just to learn to sing the one sweet song. No price in tears would have been too great to pay to be the author, for example, of the twenty third psalm, or "Rock of Ages, cleft for me." Think of the things Peter left—but was the price he paid too great? Let no one dread any suffering he may be called to endure, if thereby he becomes able to be a blessing to other lives, or leaves behind anything that will make blessings which shall enrich the earth, fruits which shall feed men's hunger.

The sculptor, hewing at his marble and seeing the chips of stone flying about, said, in explanation, "While the marble wastes—the image grows." The stone unhewn cannot grow into living beauty. The life which does not suffer, which endures no pain, cannot be fashioned into the likeness of Christ. *Simon* can become *Peter* only through *chisel* work. The marble must waste—that the image may grow. "The highest beauty is *beauty of character*, and the *chiseling of pain* completes it."

Chapter 12

People as Means of Grace

We speak of certain religious exercises as means of grace. Prayer is one of these. When we pray we stand in the very presence of God. We do not see any form—but faith makes us conscious of the shining of his face, and we cannot but be affected. We read of Moses, that when he had been long in the mountain with God and then came back to the people, that his face shone. In one of the Psalms it is said that God's people looked unto him—and were radiant. *Being with God makes us like God.* The Bible also is a means of grace. As we read its words and think upon them their revealings, their counsels, and commands, their promises and comforts bring the life of God himself into contact with our lives, and we are helped, quickened, strengthened, and made better. Whatever in our experiences brings us under the influence of God and leads us into holier life—is a means of grace to us. This is the meaning of Christian worship. More than we realize, *people* also are means of grace to us. We get our best lessons from men; we are most deeply influenced by our contacts with them. "Evil companionships corrupt good morals." We know how being with good people in intimate relations makes us better.

Many of us know a few people at least who have a strange influence over us for good. To be with them for an hour or even for a few minutes lifts us up into a new atmosphere and makes us want to live a better life.

One of the finest tests of character—is the effect a life has on other lives. There are certain people who make you desire to be gentle, kindly, thoughtful; and there are others who stir up evil desires in you, who make you bitter, resentful, who provoke you to anger and all unholiness. *The Christian should seek to be so full of spiritual influence, that all his words, his life, his conduct, shall be Christlike.*

Paul wrote of certain friends whom he hoped to visit, "I long to see you—that I may impart unto you some spiritual gift." Could there be a more fitting wish than this in the heart of one friend for another? If this were always our desire when we were about to visit another, what blessings would we carry in our friendships wherever we go! We are not aware in how large a measure God sends spiritual gifts to men through other men. When he would help one of his children in some way he does not send an angel—but he sends a friend.

One reason for the incarnation, was that only thus could God get near to us, near enough to give us the blessing we need. If he had come in Sinai's splendors, the glory would have so dazzled our eyes that we could not have endured to look upon him. So he came instead in a sweet, gentle, beautiful human life. What was true of this largest of all divine manifestations is true in lesser ways of all heavenly revealing. God does not open a window in heaven that we may look in and see his face; he shows us a glimpse of heaven in some sweet home. Christ does not come down and walk again in person upon our streets that we may see him as the disciples saw him. He makes himself known to us in and through the lives of his friends. Even as in a dewdrop, quivering on leaf or grass blade, on a summer's morning, one can see the whole expanse of the blue sky mirrored, so in the lowliest life of a true believer there is a mirroring, though dim and imperfect, of the brightness of God's glory.

Thus God reveals his love to a child through the love of the mother. Thus the mother is the first means of grace to her child. She is the earliest interpreter to it of God's love and tenderness, of his thoughtfulness and care, of his holiness and purity. In wonderful ways also are children means of grace to their parents. A prayerful father and mother learn more of the love of God and of God's fatherhood as they bend over their first-born child, or hold it in their arms—than ever they learned before from teachers and from books—even from the Bible.

In other ways, too, is a child a means of grace to its parents. Jesus set a little child in the midst of his disciples and bade them learn from it lessons of humility and simplicity. Every child that grows up in a true home, is a constant teacher, and its opening life, like a rosebud in its unfolding, pours beauty and sweetness all about. Many a home has been transformed by the unconscious ministry of a little child.

Children are means of grace to parents, also, in the very care and anxiety which they cause. They bring trouble as well as comfort. We have to work the harder to make provision for them. We have to deny ourselves when they come, and begin to live for them. They cost us anxieties, too—sleepless nights, ofttimes, when they are sick, days of weariness when a thousand things have to be done for them. Then we have to plan for them, think of their education and training, and teach them to look after the formation of their habits. In many cases, too, they cause distress by their waywardness. In many homes the sorrow over *living* children is greater far—than was the grief from the death of those who have passed from our presence.

Yet it is in these very experiences, that our children become specially means of grace to us. We learn lessons of patience in our care for them. We are trained to unselfishness as, under the pressure of love, we are all the while denying ourselves and making personal sacrifices for them. We are trained to gentler, softer moods— as we witness their sufferings and as our hearts are pained by our concerns on their behalf. Our distress as we look upon them in their struggles and temptations and are grieved by their heedlessness and waywardness works its discipline in our lives, teaching us compassion and faith as we cry to God for them. There are really no such growing times in the lives of true Christian parents as when they are bringing up their children, if they learn their lessons.

Every life, old or young, that touches ours is meant to be a means of grace to us. The poet said, "I am a part of all that I have met." He meant that every other life which had touched him had left something of itself in him. Ever bit of conversation we have with another gives us something we shall always keep. We learn many of our best lessons from our casual associations with our fellows. Every line of moral beauty in a regenerated life—is a mirroring of a fragment, at least, of the image of God, on which our eyes may look, absorbing its loveliness. Every Christian life is in an imperfect measure, yet, truly, a new incarnation. Every believer may say, "Christ lives in me." We live every day in close and intimate relations with people who bear something of God's likeness. The good and the holy, therefore, are means of grace to us because they help to interpret to us the divine beauty. In sympathetic companionship with them, we are made conversant with holiness in practical life. God comes down out of the inaccessible light and reveals himself in the human experiences of those with whom we are walking or working.

If living in direct companionship with God seems too high an experience to be possible for us, it is possible for us to live with those who do have close fellowship with him. Converse with those who live near to Christ cannot but enrich our knowledge of divine things and elevate the tone of our lives.

Even the *faults* of those with whom we come in contact may be means of grace to us. It is harder to live with disagreeable people than with those who are congenial and sweet—the very hardness becomes a splendid discipline to us and helps to develop in us the grace of patience. Having to live or work with irritable, quick tempered people may train us to self-control in speech, teaching us either to be silent under provocation, or else to give the soft answer which turns away wrath. Socrates said he married Xantippe and endured her temper, for the self discipline he found in the experience. It would not be well to advise any man to marry such a woman for the purpose of the discipline he would get; yet if by accident a man finds himself unhappily yoked to a Xantippe, and wants to turn his misfortune to good, this is the way he may do it. In any case the disagreeable people, the unreasonable people, the unlikable people with whom we find ourselves associated in the contacts of business or society—may thus in indirect ways do a great deal toward making us better.

Enemies also may prove means of grace. For one thing, they give us a chance to practice one of the hardest lessons the Master gives us to learn—to love our enemies. When those who dislike us say unkind or bitter things about us—if we find that what they say is in any measure true, we should mend our ways. If what they say is false, we should be comforted by the beatitude for those whom men reproach and persecute and against whom they say all manner of evil falsely, for the Master's sake.

Thus on all sides we find that we may get good from those about us. From the holy and saintly—we may get inspirations toward better things and be lifted up perceptibly toward goodness and saintliness. From the gentle and the loving—we receive softening influence which melts our cold winter into the genial glow of summer. From the crude and the quarrelsome—we get self discipline in our continued effort to live peaceably with such people, despite their disagreeableness and their disposition to contention. Friction polishes not metals only—but *characters* also. Iron sharpens iron; life sharpens life. People are means of grace to us.

We may grow, therefore, as Christians, in our own place among people. *Solitariness* is not good. In the broader as well as in the narrower sense—it is not good for man to be alone. Every life needs solitude at times; we should get into each of our busy days, times of silence when human presences shall be shut away, and we shall be alone with God. We need such hours for quiet thought, for communion with Christ, for spiritual feeding, for the drawing of blessing and holy influences down from heaven to replenish the waste produced by life's toil, struggle, and sorrow. There is a time for being alone. But we should not seek to live always nor usually in this way. *Life in solitude grows selfish.* The weeds of evil desire and unhealthy emotion, flourish in solitariness.

We need to live among people, that by the contacts, the best things in us may be drawn out in thought and care and service for others. It is by no means a good thing for us to live in such conditions that we are not required to think of others, to make self-denials for others, to live for others, not for ourselves. The greater and more constant the pressure in life toward unselfishness, toward looking out and not in, and lending a hand, the better for the true growth and development of our lives. We never become unselfish, but under conditions which compel us to live unselfishly. If we live—as we may live—with heart and life open to every good influence, we get some blessing, some inspiration, some touch of beauty, some new drawing out of latent life, some fresh uplift, from every person we meet, even casually. There is no life with which we come in contact, which may not bring us some message from God—or by its very faults and infirmities help to disciple us into stronger, calmer, deeper, truer life, and thus become to us a means of grace.

Chapter 13

What Christ is to me

The title of the chapter is important. It is not, "What Christ Is," but "What Christ is *to me.*" *He* may be, in our thought, a most glorious person, with all the honor claimed for him in the New Testament—and yet be nothing at all to *me* personally. He may be a great Savior—and not be *my* Savior. He may be a wonderful Friend— and yet his friendship means nothing whatever to me. The twenty third psalm is an exquisite little poem. It is dear to the hearts of millions of believers. But it would not be the same if it began, "The Lord is *a* Shepherd." It is the word "my" which gives it its dearness. So it would not be the same if the title of this chapter were, "What Christ Is." It might depict his character in glorious words. He is the Son of God, deity shining in every line. He is the King of kings, worthy of the worship and adoration of the highest beings in the world. He has all divine excellences. It was no robbery of God, for Jesus Christ to claim to be equal with God. But we may believe all that the creeds of Christendom assert regarding him—and yet receive no blessing from him.

The question, *what Christ is to us*, starts in our hearts infinite thoughts of love, of mercy, of comfort. How can we ever tell what he has been to us? We may think of what he has done for us as our Savior. This opens a vista back to the heart of God— and into eternity. We cannot understand what the Bible tells us of the kingdom prepared for us from the foundation of the world, of our names having been written in the Lamb's book of life from the foundation of the world. Whatever these and other such words mean, they certainly suggest that we have been in the heart of God from the eternal past. There is something bewildering in this revealing—that Christ thought about us before we were made.

We may think also of what Christ is to us in personal ways. For one thing, he is our Friend, and he calls us his friends. Then need of friendship is the deepest need of life. Every heart cries out for it. Christ spoke no other word to his disciples which meant more to them than when he said, "I will be your friend." A young man, a teacher in a mission school in the South, said these words to a boy who had been brought up in the darkest ignorance, who had never heard a kind word before, and who had never had a friend. The words fell upon the boy's ear, like something spoken from heaven. Some days afterward the boy lingered about until the teacher was alone, and said to him, "Did you mean what you said the other day—that you would be my friend?" The teacher assured him that he did. "If you will be my friend," the boy said, "I can become a man." It was the beginning of a new life to the boy.

Hundreds of people in barren conditions never hear such a word from any lips and are starved to death for love. Human friends have brought life, joy, hope, and marvelous uplifting to countless lives just by saying, "I will be your friend." Nothing you can do for the world could mean half so much to men—as just going among them and in reality becoming their friend. There are great men, with noble gifts and splendid qualities, who have learned the secret of loving others, who are doing marvelous good among their fellows, not by giving them anything, nor by doing anything for them—but just by being a friend to them.

There never was any other man who wrought such a ministry of friendship as *Christ* has wrought through the centuries. He is always coming to men and saying, "I am your friend." That was the way he saved Simon, making of him the great apostle whose name is known through the world. That was the way he took the youth John, becoming his friend, putting a glorious ideal into his heart, and making him ultimately the apostle of love. It is this blessed friendship that, all the Christian centuries, has been touching lives everywhere with its own spirit of unselfishness and service. There are many pictures of Jesus in the Gospels—but perhaps there is no one more suggestive of his real character, than the one which shows him girt with a towel, holding the basin and washing the disciples' feet. There is nothing Jesus would not do—no sacrifice he would not make—no humbling of himself to which he would not stoop—in doing the part of a friend.

Dr. Watson tells of once hearing a plain sermon in a little country church. It was a layman, a farmer, who preached—but Dr. Watson says he never heard so impressive an ending to any sermon as he heard that day. After a fervent presentation of the Gospel, the preacher said with great earnestness: "My friends, why is it that I go on, preaching to you, week by week? It is just this—because I can't eat my bread alone." That is the Master's own burden—his heart is breaking to have men share with him the blessings of life. He cannot bear to be alone in his joy. There is no surer test of love for Christ—than the longing to have others love him.

When we receive Christ's friendship and love into our hearts, infinite possibilities of blessing are ours. Christ becomes our teacher, our guide, our burden-bearer, our very life. We are transformed through his influence. Loving him makes our dull lives radiant. A missionary teacher of Tokyo tells of a Japanese woman who came to speak about having her daughter received into the school for girls which the teacher was conducting. She asked if only beautiful girls were admitted. "No," was the reply; "we take any girl who desires to come." "But," continued the woman, "All your girls that I have seen are very beautiful." The teacher replied, "We tell them of Christ, and seek to have them take him into their hearts, and this makes their faces lovely." The woman answered, "Well, I do not want my daughter to become a Christian—but I am going to send her to your school to get that look in her face."

Christ is the sweetener and beautifier of the lives and the very faces of those who become his friends. He gives them peace, and peace brightens and transforms their features. He teaches them love, and love makes them beautiful. A girl who was very homely, so homely that even her mother told her she never would have any friends, determined to make her life so winning by its *graciousness* and its ministry of *kindness,* that her homeliness would be forgotten. She gave herself to Christ in a simple and complete devotion and sought to be wholly under his influence. She then devoted herself to the helping and serving of others, until she was known everywhere as the *angel* of the town where she lived. Her ugliness of features, was forgotten, in the beauty of her disposition and life. That is what having Christ for a friend does for those who yield themselves to his transforming influence.

In no other experience in life is the blessing of the friendship of Christ more wonderful than in the times of affliction and trouble. "It is worth our thought," says Huntington, "how small the audience would be that would assemble weekly, to listen to a gospel that had nothing to say to sufferers. Poor, weak, broken hearts, staggering under their loads, would refuse a comforter who had never wept himself, nor remembered that his followers must weep. A religion that addressed itself only to those who are in a state of comfort would be like a system of navigation calculated only for clear weather, and giving no aid when night and cloud have wiped out all way marks from earth and sky, and the tempest shrieks in the darkness over an unknown sea."

The Bible is a great book of comfort. The heart of Christ was wonderfully sensitive to suffering. He was called a man of sorrows, and it is said that he was acquainted with grief, that is, with all phases of grief. We may know a little of pain, one phase of suffering—but Christ knew the whole field of grief. Yet the griefs of the world did not make him bitter. One of the dangers with us—is that we shall receive hurt from life's trials, shall be hardened by them. Christ received no harm from anything which he suffered. He came through all painful experience with the gentleness of his heart still gentler. He never complained of God, charging him with unkindness or saying he did not care when his children suffered.

We never can know in the present world, what we owe to the hard things in our lives, what pain and suffering do for us. Christ makes these experiences a *school of blessing and good* for us. He changes our crown of thorns—into a garland of roses. We have to meet hard things in our experiences—but it is never God's will that we shall be hurt by them; he wants us always to be helped by them, made better, our lives enriched.

In Barrie's book, is a chapter with the suggestive title, "How My Mother Got Her Soft Face." She got it through suffering. Her boy was hurt. News had come that he was near death, far away from home, and the mother set out to go to him, hoping to reach him in time to minister to him and comfort him. Her ticket was bought; she had bidden the other children goodbye at the station. Then the father came out of the little telegraph office and said sadly, "He's gone," and they all went home again. She was another woman ever after, however, a better woman, gentler. Barrie says, "That is how my mother got her soft face and her pathetic ways and her large charity, and why other mothers run to her when they have lost a child." There are many other mothers who have got soft faces in the same way. They have had very hard troubles to bear—but their lives have been made more beautiful by the hardness. That is part of what Christ is to us—he leads us through pain and loss— but our faces grow softer.

What is Christ to us in the development of our lives? A woman spent the summer in the mountains and brought home with her in the autumn some pieces of lovely moss. She put it in her conservatory, and in the warmth of the place, a multitude of beautiful little flowers came up among the moss. There are in us possibilities which, in common experiences are not brought out—but when the warmth and light of the love of God pour about them they are wooed forth. The poet, when asked what Christ was to him; pointed to a rose bush near by, full of glorious roses. "What the sun is to this rose bush," he said, "Christ is to me." Whatever is lovely in our lives has been brought out by the warmth of Christ's love touching us and calling out the loveliness. We do not realize all that Christ may be to us, what undeveloped beauty there is in our natures that he will bring out, if we yield ourselves to him.

What is Christ to us in our hope for the future? The veil that hides the eternal world is not lifted here—but we have visions of something very wonderful waiting for us. "It is not yet made manifest what we shall be. We know that, if he shall be manifested, we shall be like him; for we shall see him even as he is." That is enough for us to want to know. A Christian woman was speaking of a saintly man who was for many years the superintendent of a large city Sunday school. He was a man of most gentle spirit. He loved the children with a love that made them most dear to him. When he lay in his coffin, the members of his Sunday school passed by to look at his face in their last farewell, and every child laid a flower on his breast, until he was literally buried beneath the sweet blossoms. Speaking of his death, the woman said, "He must have passed right into the bosom of Jesus, he was so true, so holy, so Christlike." That is what death means to one who has followed Christ faithfully.

When the news went out that Phillips Brooks was dead, the mother in one home where he was most dear, told her little daughter that her good friend was gone. She had dreaded to break the news to her lest her grief might be overpowering—but the child only exclaimed, "Oh, mother, how glad the angels must be to have him in heaven!"

It is sweet to think, that when we go away from the dear love of earth, we shall be with Christ, lying on his bosom, welcomed by angels and by waiting saints. Christ is everything beautiful to us here: there he will be infinitely more to us.

Chapter 14

Our Unanswered Prayers

In one of our hymns there is a line which runs, *"Teach me the patience of unanswered prayer."* The writer's thought is patience in waiting when our prayer seems not to be answered. The answer may be only *delayed*. Sometimes it takes a long time for God to give us the answer we seek. We can think of several possible reasons.

Perhaps the thing we seek cannot be prepared for us at once. God does not work *unnecessary miracles*. The economy of supernatural acts is to be noted in our Lord's life. He had all power and could do anything. Nature's limitations set no trammels for him. He could have changed water into wine whenever he wished to do so—but he did it only once. He could have make bread from stones—but he never did. He wrought a number of miracles—but he did thousands of deeds of common kindness when there was no necessity for supernatural acts. Some of the prayers we make, could be answered at once only by miracle. It is not the will of God to give us the answer in that way, and so he requires us to wait while he prepares it for us in a natural way.

If you want an oak tree to grow on your lawn and pray for it, God will not cause it to spring up overnight. He will bid you drop an acorn in the place where you want to have the tree, and it will grow as trees always grow and your prayer will be answered—but not fully for a long time. You will need the patience of unanswered prayer.

A young man has a desire to do great things. He has high ideals and is ambitious to achieve noble things. God may be willing to give him what he wishes—but not instantaneously. The young man needs to have his mental faculties developed and trained in order that he may be able to accomplish the great things he desires to do. Long after, in the years of maturity, he may achieve the thing he prayed in youth to be able to do. But now the prayer offered so importunately seems not to be answered. Really, however, it is answered as soon as God could answer it. We need the patience of unanswered prayer while we do not seem to be receiving at all the thing we long for and ask for.

You pray to have the Christian graces in your life. You want to have joy, patience, gentleness, humility, mercifulness. But these heavenly qualities cannot be put into your life at once; they have to grow from small beginnings to perfection—but "first the blade, then the ear, then the full grain in the ear,"—but that requires a long time. It needs "the patience of unanswered prayer" in your heart, that you may not be discouraged while you wait.

Another reason for slowness in the answering of prayer, may be in ourselves. *We are not yet ready* to receive the thing we seek. There must be a work done in us, a work of preparation before the thing we seek can be given to us. A young man has a strong desire to go into a certain calling or business and prays earnestly and persistently that the way may be opened for him. But he has not now the qualification to make him successful in that business. Only by a long experience, can he be made ready for it. His prayer may seem long to be unanswered—but it needs only patience and continuance in work and prayer combined. Prayer without work would never be answered. Many prayers wait for answer for something that must be done first in us.

Our prayers for spiritual blessings cannot be answered until a great work has been wrought in us. You want to be *holy*. You are weary of sinning and grieving God. Months pass and somehow your prayer seems to have no answer. The trouble is, it can be answered only in your own heart. The evil there must be driven out. You pray to be made *gentle*. God loves to answer such a prayer—but the answer can come only through a long, slow discipline in which your old nature must be softened. You must have patience, for this great lesson is long and cannot be learned in a day. It never can come into any life as an immediate answer to prayer. It takes some people a whole lifetime to learn always to be kind, always to be gentle. But it is worth while to give even the longest lifetime to the learning of such a lesson.

But why should we pray at all—when we must win the answer by our own striving? Only with *divine help* can such prayers ever be answered. We cannot alone make ourselves gentle, or kind, or humble. These are among the things which we cannot do apart from Christ. There is a legend of an ancient church in England, which tells that while a new building was being erected, there came among the workmen a stranger and began to help them. This man always took, unasked, the hardest tasks. When a beam had been lifted to its place and was found too short, the men tried in every way to remedy the defect—but in vain. Night closed in, leaving them in great perplexity—but in the morning the beam was in its place, lengthened to the exact dimensions required. The strange workman was gone—but now the men understood that it was the Master himself who had been working with them unrecognized, supplying their lack of wisdom and strength. The legend has its teaching for us. We are not toiling*unhelped* at our work. We are not seeking the blessings of grace *unaided*. While we pray for new gifts and strive to attain them, Christ is with us, unseen, and our prayers shall not be unanswered nor our longings be unattained.

Another reason that prayers seem to remain unanswered, may be that the answers we desire and expect, would not be the *wisest* and *best*. Those who were praying and waiting for the Messiah before Jesus came, never received the answer they were looking for. They expected a Messiah who would be an earthly conqueror. Their prayers were unanswered, though the Messiah came. Many people pray for certain things which they think would be great blessings to them if they would receive them. God is willing to grant them the best gifts of his love. He does not reject their prayers. But *the things they plead for would not be the good they seek.* If they were granted to them, they would be only *empty husks*, not the corn their hunger craves. Not receiving what they so eagerly longed for, and have pleaded for so earnestly— they suppose they have prayed in vain, that God has not listened to their requests. Meanwhile, the *real good* which their hearts needed, has been coming to them continually, coming in what they regarded as unanswered prayers.

Christian life is full of just such experiences as these. We do not know what really the things are, which we need most. Our vision is limited. We are swayed by the physical. We think a certain thing, if we had it, would make us almost perfectly happy; and that if it is not given to us, no matter what other good things we may receive, we cannot be happy. So we pray with great earnestness and importunity that God will grant to us this thing which seems so essential to us. Yet we do not surely know that the thing, so desired, will prove to us the blessing which we think it will be. Many people have felt the same concerning desires they had, and have received them only to be bitterly disappointed. They found only *ashes* where they expected to find *delicious fruit*. Or they shrank from a great sorrow which they saw coming toward them, and prayed that its coming might be averted. The prayer was not granted. The sorrow came with its apparent desolation. But out of it came in the end—the greatest good for which they will praise God in eternity.

No doubt we shall some time thank God that many ardent prayers of ours were *not* granted. One man earnestly longed to enter a certain business and prayed that he might be allowed to do so. But his desire was not granted. Later he was led into another line of life in which he found an opportunity for large prosperity and for great usefulness.

In a beautiful home a little child lay very sick. The young parents had once been active Christians—but in their first wedded happiness they had given up Christ, and had now no place in their home for God. Their happiness seemed complete when the baby came. Radiant were the days that followed. Their joy knew no bounds. Then the baby fell very sick. In their alarm the parents sought the offices of religion, and earnest and continued prayer were offered by the little one's bedside. Great physicians consulted together and all that science could do was done. But the baby died. "God did not answer our prayers," the parents said, and they complained bitterly.

Years afterward the father wrote these words to a friend: "I believe now that if God had granted my ardent prayers for the life of my beautiful first born son when he was taken sick at nine months old, I never would have been the man I am now; I would have remained the godless man I had then become. But when I stood with my despairing wife beside our dead baby, even feeling bitter toward God because he had not heard our cries, I remembered how I had departed from God—and returned to him with penitence and confession. The death of my boy brought me back to Christ." The prayers seemed unanswered. At least the answer came not as the father wished—but God's way was better. The boy's life was not spared—but the father was saved.

There are many who tell us that their prayers are unanswered, who, if they knew the whole story of these prayers, would see that God showed his love and wisdom far more wondrously in *denying* their requests—than if he had *given* them just what they pleaded for so earnestly. The prayers were really answered—but in God's way—not in their way—and God's way was better. God is too good to give us a stone, however earnestly we cry to him for it, thinking it is bread. Instead, he will disappoint us by giving us bread.

One of the blessings we need therefore to pray for continually, is "the patience of unanswered prayer," that we may be saved from *impatience*, as our prayers seem so long in being answered; or from *disappointment*, when they seem not to be answered at all. No true prayer ever is unanswered. It may bring no apparent answer at once—but it still waits before God and is not forgotten. The answer may come in some other form. When Paul prayed that his distressing "thorn in the flesh" might be removed, his request was not granted—but instead he received *more grace*. That is, to compensate for the pain that he must keep—he would have more of Christ. Many times pain is the price God's children have to pay for spiritual strength. We may be sure at least—that the prayers are never unanswered. They bring answers in some form at least.

Chapter 15

The Outflow of Song

In one of his epistles, Paul gives an interesting suggestion for a beautiful life. He says, "let the word of Christ dwell in you richly; in all wisdom teaching and admonishing one another with psalms and hymns and spiritual songs." The point to be noted is that the dwelling of the word of Christ in the heart produces a musical outflow, a life of song— "psalms and hymns and spiritual songs."

The words suggest, in general, good and beautiful lives. Every such life is a song. In another of his epistles Paul says, "We are God's workmanship," and commentators tell us that the word *workmanship* means poem. "We are God's *poem*."

Poetry is supposed to be more beautiful than prose. It is characterized by fineness and loftiness of thought, and by charm and beauty of expression. It is not merely something in rhyme, as some writers seem to think. There are rhymes which do not make poetry. A life that is God's poem, should be very beautiful. We may not be able to *write* poetry, like Tennyson's, which will charm by its music and by its beauty—but we may *live* poems. We may not be able to *write* twenty-third psalms—but we can*live* them. We may make our life a sweet song. We do not need to be poets to do this. A very prosaic man may so live—that gentle music shall breathe from his life all his days. He needs only to be true and just and loving. There are people whose lives are so sweet, so patient, so gentle, so thoughtful, so unselfish, so helpful, and so full of quiet goodness, that they are exquisite poems. They may be plain, simple, without fame, without show, without brilliance—but the marks of God's hands are on them!

We are God's poems. Every beautiful life is a poem. There are people, living in conditions of hardness; whose lives we would say could not possibly have any music in them. Their circumstances are utterly prosaic, with no room for sentiment. Even home tenderness would appear to be impossible in their experiences of toil and pinching poverty. Yet even such lives as these, doomed to heavy work and dreary hardship, or constant pain, ofttimes do become poems in their beauty and winningness. There are many men who never have an hour's leisure or a bit of luxury in all their years, who yet please God continually by their faithfulness, their patience, their contentment, the peace of Christ in their hearts—whose lives are lovely songs. You may not find these poems in homes of luxury and splendor. There is more joy ofttimes in the plain cottages of those who are poor and love God—than in the mansions of the rich who care not for God. Their *lives* are poems. We find them as we go about these days, sometimes in sick rooms—they are uncomplaining, unmurmuring, singing in suffering; sometimes in experiences of loss and poverty—they are patient and trusting. In many a lowly home you will find poems finer than ever you read in books. The mother of Goethe used to say that when her son had a grief he turned it into a poem. He who knows the secret, may turn all his troubles into poems.

Another meaning of this description—"psalms and hymns and spiritual songs"—is that our lives should be **joyous**. God wants them to be songs. He wants them to be pure, sweet, gentle, and kind.

We get music into our lives, when we *live sweetly* in hard circumstances and amid trying experiences. Anybody ought to be able to live songfully in summer days, with flowers strewn all along the path, with only gladness on every hand. But to live rejoicingly in the midst of discouragements, hindrances, and all manner of trouble, is a truer test. The newspapers some time ago, told of a ship coming over from Germany in midwinter with a cargo of many thousand song birds. At the beginning of the voyage the weather was warm and clear. Not a bird sang in those days. Not a note of music was heard. The birds all seemed depressed and unhappy. But about the third day out it began to get colder, and soon the wind was blowing stiffly and there was stormy weather. Then the birds began to sing. Soon all the twenty five or thirty thousand little throats were pouring out song.

People often say that if they had only ease and luxury all the time—costly furniture, sumptuous meals, automobiles—that they would be gladder and would live more sweetly. But if our hearts are right—we should sing all the better, the more joyously—when life is hard, when we have heavy tasks and sharp trials, keen losses and bitter sorrows. An invalid who loved to hear the birds sing at her window said she liked the robin best of all the birds—because the robin sang in the rain.

There are some people who have not learned to *sing in the rain*. They are easily discouraged. Nehemiah wanted the Jews, who were rebuilding the Temple, to rejoice. They were disheartened, and he wanted them to sing. "The joy of the Lord is your strength," he told them. They would be stronger if they would sing. They would get on better with their building. That is what God wants us to do. He does not want them ever to be gloomy or unhappy. When the word of Christ richly dwells in them—the result will be "psalms and hymns and spiritual songs." Paul puts it thus in another of his epistles, when he says, "Rejoice in the Lord always: again I will say, Rejoice." That is, if you are a Christian, you should be a happy one. An unhappy Christian is not doing honor to Christ.

Yet, somehow, many Christians seem not to understand this. Not everyone who bears the name of Christ, sings psalms and hymns and spiritual songs in his daily life. There are Christians who are not always sweet and songful. Some are gloomy, unsympathetic, and cynical. One man said of his neighbor, "I am sure he is a Christian—but he is a disagreeable one." Of another man, in contrast with this one, a neighbor said that other people learned at his feet the kindliness, the gentleness, the sympathy, the considerateness of Christ himself. He lived psalms and hymns wherever he went.

God wants our lives to be songs every day, every night, everywhere. He makes the music bars for us and we are to set the notes on them. The notes are our obediences. God's will is an anthem set for us to sing. There never would be any discords in the music, if we always did God's will, and did it sweetly. Any disobedience, however, any wrong thing we do, any unloving thing, will break the harmony. A perfectly holy life would be a faultless song.

If we would have such musical outflow in our lives—we must keep love in our hearts. Nothing but love makes music. Hate is always discordant. One of the finest things the world has heard in recent days, is the news of the movement for a treaty of international peace. This is a sign of the coming fulfillment of the glorious reign of peace of which the prophets spoke, when wars shall cease, when the nations shall beat their swords into ploughshares, and their spears into pruning hooks.

There is a picture called 'Peace'. It is of a quiet meadow scene, with a cannon lying amid the grass and flowers. A lamb is feeding there. The warlike gun is now part of the picture of peace. But the gun, even resting, spoils the picture. Here is something better. A tourist tells of visiting a little village in Germany where the church bells that rang on Sundays were made of cannon that had been used in the Prussian War. Instead of belching forth death, the guns now proclaim peace. Dr. Jowett tells of a shop where he saw workmen making bombshells into pots and dishes. That is precisely what the prophet foretold concerning the changing of implements of war into the implements of peace. Every Christian should help to make it true, that nations shall learn war no more. Then would the angel's song, "Peace on earth, good will to men," become part of the glad life of the world.

This life of song—psalms and hymns and spiritual songs—should be the music of every Christian community, of every Christian home. How much broken music there is in many homes! Instruments out of tune make discourdance in the music. Musical people speak of certain harsh sounds in instruments as 'wolf notes'. There are wolf notes in the music of some homes where violent tempers are indulged, where jealousy, hate, lust, the wild utterances of passion, mar the music.

The word of Christ dwelling in the heart would produce a life of song—"psalms and hymns and spiritual songs"—every jarring discord hushed into harmony. That is what Christian peace is. That is what love is.

There is One who can take our lives, with all their jangled chords, their faults and sin, and bring from them the music of love, joy, and peace. There is an old legend of an instrument that long hung silent upon a castle wall. Its strings were broken. It was covered with dust. No one understood it, and no one could put it in order. Many had tried to do this—but had failed. No one could play on it. But one day a stranger came to the castle. He saw the instrument on the wall. Taking it down, he quickly brushed the cobwebs from it, gently reset the broken strings, and then played upon it, making marvelous music.

This is a parable of what Christ does for those who believe on him. Every human life in its natural state is a harp, tarnished by sin, its strings broken. It is capable, however, of giving forth music marvelously rich and beautiful. But first it must be restored, its strings reset; and the only one who can do this is the master of the harp, the Lord Jesus Christ. Only he can bring the jangled chords of our lives into tune, so that when played upon—they shall give forth rich music. If we would have our lives become songs, we must surrender our hearts to Christ—that he may repair and restore them. Then we shall be able to make music, not in our individual lives only—but in whatever relations our lot may be cast, and in whatever circumstances it may fall to us to dwell.

Let the word of Christ dwell in you richly—and then songs will pour out in all your experiences. One sat before an open fire, where green logs were burning, and listened to the weird music that the fire brought out, and spoke this little parable: "When the logs were green trees in the woods the birds sat on the branches and twittered and sang, and the notes sank away into the wood of the trees and hid there. And now the *fire* brings out the hidden music." Just so, we may let the words of Christ sink into our hearts as we read them, ponder them, love them. Then, wherever we go, whatever we do, whatever our experiences are, if we suffer, if we have struggle, if we have sorrow, if we have joy, the music will come out in psalms and hymns and spiritual songs!

Chapter 16

Seeing the Sunny Side

Thankfulness is one of the cardinal virtues. One of the finest marks in a noble life, is perennial praise. Yet this spirit is rare. It is the exception to find among people, one who sees something to thank God for in all life's circumstances. The great majority of people are *grumblers*. They seem to be looking always for unpleasant things. For example, there appears to be a very common disposition to see the dark and discouraging side of Christian life and Christian work. There appears to be just now a chronic tendency in the religious press and among Christian ministers to think and talk dishearteningly of the condition of things in the churches. It has been shown over and over again that there has been a marvelous progress in the influence of Christianity within a century. But in some way the croakers give out the impression that religion is waning, that the churches are dwindling and dying out, that very few men are interested in the work of Christ. The truth of the assertions is taken for granted, and ministers and church officers, as well as the rank and file, go about bemoaning the sad condition of things and wondering what is going to be the end of it all.

Not long ago, somebody sent out a scare article about the exhaustion of the material in the sun. This material is being consumed at an amazing rate, and the writer showed that in a certain number of thousands of years the sun will be burnt out, becoming only a big, cold, dark cinder, like the moon. What shall we do then? There is even less to alarm any thoughtful person in the talk about the dying out of Christianity than in the assertion that the sun is burning out. Those who are pessimistic about the general decadence of Christianity, ought to look up the statistics, ought to read the reports of the wonderful work and progress of Young Men's Christian Associations, of the Laymen's Missionary Movement, of the great missionary conventions and of the story of the Christian work that is being done in the cities, and the tremendous things the Sunday schools are doing throughout he world.

Such a view of the situation, ought to set in motion a new tide of cheer, hope, encouragement, in the churches and among Christian people. Instead of deploring the dying out of Christian life and activity—there should begin now a new era of gladness, of enthusiasm, of praise, for the great things the church is doing.

The question was asked of two church officers, "How are matters in your church this year?" The first spoke discouragingly. The church to which he belonged seemed dead, he said. The attendance was not large. The Sunday school had fallen off. The prayer meetings were only a handful. The men in the membership appeared indifferent. Even the pastor did not seem as enthusiastic as he used to be. The whole tone of the good man's talk was pessimistic. There was not a glad, cheerful, praising word in all he said.

The other man, to the same question, answered with enthusiasm. The meetings were full. The pastor was working with earnestness and hope. Everybody was eager to work. A tone of thanksgiving ran through all his words. A church with such sunshiny men for its officers will have twice the success and blessing that a church can have whose officers are gloomy, disheartened, and hopeless.

But it is not in religious life and work alone, that there is so much lack of cheer and hope. In all lines of life one finds the same spirit. In many homes there is almost an entire absence of the thanksgiving spirit. A *shadow* rests on all the life. There is an immense amount of *whining* heard. Nothing is quite satisfactory. There is little singing. The quest seems to be searching for spots and mistakes of others, something to blame and condemn. How much better it would be, how much more of heaven we would get into our homes if we would train ourselves to find the beautiful things and good things in each other, and in all our experiences and circumstances! Anybody can find fault—it takes no genius to do this. Genius is far better shown in finding something to praise and commend in imperfect people, in hard conditions.

Here is a paragraph from someone, which suggests a better way at home, than the complaining way: "She knew how to forget disagreeable things. She kept her nerves well in hand, and inflicted them on no one. She mastered the *art of saying pleasant things*. She did not expect too much from her friends. She made whatever work came to her, congenial. She relieved the miserable, and sympathized with the sorrowful. She never forgot that kind words, and a gentle smile cost nothing—were a rare priceless treasures to the discouraged. She did unto others as she would be done by, and now that old age has come to her, and there is a halo of white hair about her head, she is beloved and revered. This is the secret of a long life and a happy one."

Everything depends upon the way we look at things, whether we see *shadow* or *brightness* in them. Miss Mulock, in one of her books, tells of a gentleman and a lady who were passing through a timber yard, by a dirty, foul smelling river. The lady remarked, "How good these pine boards smell!" "Pine boards!" exclaimed her companion. "Just smell this foul river!" "No, thank you," the lady replied, "I prefer to smell the pine boards."

The woman was wiser than her friend. She was entirely right in her way of dealing with the conditions. Both the foul river and the fragrant pine boards were present in the surroundings, and it was a question which of the two she should allow to impress her. She had the happy faculty of trying always to find the most cheerful quality in her circumstances, and so it was the sweetness of the air, and not the foulness of the river—that she chose to find in her walk that day. We may train ourselves always to make the same distinction and choice in what we find in our circumstances—to see the beauty, the pleasure, the charm—rather than the ugliness, the pain, the disagreeableness. Too many people never see anything but the discouraging aspect of things, so they are never in a really thankful mood. A little *sunny hearted mind set,* would make a world of difference in the lives of a great many men and women.

Things are not going so terribly wrong, after all, as the *croakers* think they are. There are always a lot of things that are good and comfortable—far more indeed than there are painful and unhappy things. We have only to make up our minds to find the*bright* spots and make the most of them. One January day, when the house was cold, the dog was trying to be as warm as he could. He was lying in the parlor, which was not heated. Along in the forenoon a beam of sunshine came through the blinds and fell on the floor, making a patch of sunshine on the carpet. The drowsy, shivering dog saw it, got up, stretched himself, walked to the spot and lay down in the bright place. Instead of staying in the chill and darkness, when he saw even an inch or two of warmth and light—he appropriated it. There is not one of us who on the gloomiest day of his life cannot find at least a square yard of sunshine somewhere. Let us go and lie down in it and take the comfort we can find in it.

There are a good many people who make life harder for others by indulging in this habit of always taking disheartening views and always saying dispiriting things. They call on a sick friend and tell him how ill he looks, and the man is worse all day afterwards. They meet one who is in some trouble and sympathize with him in such a way that the trouble seems ten times greater. They come upon a neighbor who is discouraged, and they talk with him until he is almost in despair. They think they are showing a kindly spirit in all this—but they are really only *adding to the burdens* of their friends and making life infinitely harder for them.

There are men in these very days, who are evermore putting *doubts* into the minds of others and raising *questions* which only cause fear and uncertainty. We ought not to add to the spiritual perplexity of men by holding up shreds of torn pages, as if our Christianity were something riddled to tatters by those who have thrown away their childhood faith. "Give me your beliefs," said Goethe; "I have doubts enough of my own." So people are saying to us, "Give us your hopes, your joys, your sunshine, your confidence, your uplifting faiths; we have sorrows, tears, clouds, fears, uncertainties enough of our own." People need to be *helped*—not *hindered.*

Nine of every ten people you will meet tomorrow will be carrying as many and as heavy loads as they can possibly carry. They will not need to have their burdens lifted away—that would not be the truest kindness to them; their burdens are God's gifts, and in bearing them they are to grow; but they will need cheer and strength— that they may walk steadily, bravely, and unfalteringly under their loads. There is nothing that the world needs—as much as cheer. A discourager is always a hinderer. He makes it harder for everyone to be good, to be strong and true. An encourager is a friend of men. He is the blessing of his race. He is a benefactor. He is an inspirer of joy. He is a fountain of love. Christ himself was always an encourager. He never spoke a discouraging word to any man or woman. In the most hopeless life he saw the possibilities of heavenly glory. We must be like our Master and must live like him if we would do our part in making the world better, and putting sunshine into it.

Let us then cease forever our miserable habit of prophesying evil. The way to get more people to go to church, is to make our churches sunnier, more cheerful, more human, more helpful, more like sweet and holy homes. The way to get more good into the world, is to stop our ungrateful fault finding and discouragement, and begin to help everybody to be good and brave and true. Thanksgiving is the word; if we have thanksgiving lives we shall have lives of blessing, and everyone who knows us will begin to love Christ more and love his neighbor more.

Chapter 17

The Story of the Folded Hands

One of the finest secrets of success, lies in *finding one's true place*. Many a life with splendid qualities comes to little use, because it fails in this regard. Many a man, who struggles through years in a profession and never rises to distinction, never accomplishes anything that gives satisfaction to himself or to his friends, would have won a worthy record in some other line of business or in a trade. There are men who imagine they have talents for almost any kind of calling, that they could do almost anything that man can do. But the truth is, that no man has in him a universality of talent. Every man has a talent for something. There is one thing he can do well—if he trains himself for it.

Probably mothers spoil many of their children's lives, by trying to be their guide. They decide that their boys shall be ministers or doctors or artists or inventors, and teach them in infancy what they are going to be in life, regardless of what their natural gifs may be. The result is that the boys grow up without being free to think for themselves, biased and constrained toward some calling for which perhaps they have no natural fitness whatever.

There are many sad failures in life because of a wrong choice of vocation. Some men stumble along, trying one thing and failing, then trying something else, and probably failing again and again, until half their life is gone and they are still unsettled, without a place in which they are content, or in which they are doing the work God made them to do.

It would seem to be a great blessing to masses of people if there were some way by which boys could be shown very early in their lives what they could do best, and in what calling they could make the most of their lives. But this is not the *divine* way. God leads us usually through series of *providences* and *experiences,* and in the end we seem to have to find our own way. Nevertheless, God is willing to guide us. Indeed, he has a plan for every one of our lives, something he wants us to do, a *niche* he wants us to fill, and he will show us the way to our place and to our duty.

The chief thing for us is to be willing to take the place for which he has made us—to do the work he has fitted us to do. We must be satisfied to do this, however lowly the place may be. God's place for us may not be a place of *fame*—it may be an obscure place. One of the hardest lessons we have to learn, may be the taking of an obscure place after we have been trying for a while to get into a conspicuous place and have failed in filling it. When we learn at last that we cannot do the *great* things we wanted to do, it is beautiful in us to accept our disappointment and take graciously and sweetly the lowlier place, and to begin to do the less brilliant things which we can do.

Many people are familiar with Durer's *Folded Hands*, a picture of two hands clasped as in prayer. There is a charming story of the way the famous picture came to be painted. Here is the story, as it comes to us. Whether authentic or not, it is interesting and has its lessons. It illustrates too, the lesson which has been suggested.

A good while ago, in quaint old Nuremberg, lived two boys, Franz Knigstein and Albrecht Durer. Both wished to be artists and both began to study. The parents of the boys were poor and worked hard to help their sons. Albrecht had genius but Franz had only love for art without real artistic skill. Visions of beautiful pictures haunted him—but his hand lacked the deftness to put these visions on canvas. Still, the boys both worked hard and hoped for success.

Years passed and they planned to make, each of them, an etching of our Lord's passion. When they compared their finished work, that of Franz was cold and without life, while Albrecht's was instinct with beauty and pathos. Franz saw it all, as he looked upon the two etchings, and knew now that he could never be an artist. His heart was almost broken—but he did not murmur. Only for one passionate moment he buried his face in his hands. Then he said to Albrecht, in a voice broken and sad—but full of manly courage: "The good Lord gave me no such gift as this of yours. But something he has yet for me to do. Some lowly duty is waiting somewhere for me...." "Be still! Franz, be quiet one minute," cried Albrecht, seizing pencil and paper. Franz supposed that Albrecht was putting some finishing touches to his exquisite drawing and waited patiently, his hands still clasped together. With his swift pencil Albrecht drew a few lines and showed the sketch to his friend.

"Why, those are only my hands," Franz said. "Why did you draw them?"

"I sketched them," said Albrecht, "as you stood there making the surrender of your life so nobly and bravely. I said to myself then, 'Those hands which will never paint a picture, can now most certainly make one.' I have faith in those hands, my brother-friend. They will go to men's hearts in the days to come."

Albrecht's prophecy has been fulfilled. Into the world of love and duty, there has gone the story so touching and helpful in its beautiful simplicity, and into the world of art has gone the picture—but for Albrecht's Durer's Folded Hands, are but the hands of Franz Knigstein, as they were folded that day in sweet, brave resignation when he gave up his heart's dearest wish, and yet had faith to believe that the Lord had some lowly duty worth his doing.

This story has its lessons, which it is worth our while to note and remember. For one thing, it teaches that if we cannot do the rare and beautiful things we see other people doing and aspire to do ourselves, we can at least do something that will please God and be a blessing to the world. It is not every man's mission to be a great artist. God has a plan for each life, and we best honor him when we discover what he has made us to do and then quietly and patiently do it. Albrecht Durer had the artist's gift. Franz Knigstein had love for beauty and wished to be an artist. But it became evident to him after a time of earnest, diligent trial, that he never could acquire the artist's skill. He had not the genius for it. It was no dishonor to Franz that his gifts were not equal to Albrecht's. He had not been indolent in study or work. There are men whose failure to be great is their own fault. They have never done their best. They have trifled and loitered. Some of the saddest tragedies in life are the tragedies of indolence. But Franz had done his best. Only his gift was less brilliant than his friend's. We need never feel that we have failed because another surpasses us in some particular line. If we have truly done our best, we have succeeded.

A large element in success is in being in the right place—the place for which God made us, and the place for which we have the gift. Many fail, never making anything worth while of their lives because they are trying to do something they have not the talent for doing. There are men in the professions who do not get on, yet who would have done well, achieving success, if they had found the right place–the place for which they had talents. It is most important, therefore, that young men in choosing their occupation and their work shall seek divine guidance and do what they were made to do, what they can do. It is better to stand in a high rank in a lowly occupation than utterly fail in a profession or calling which seems to be more honorable. It is not his occupation which gives dignity to a man—but the *way* he fills it; not the things he does—but he way he does them.

Another lesson from the Folded Hands, is that when it becomes evident to anyone that he cannot do the things he has set his heart on doing, when he discovers that he cannot win the prize—that he should submit courageously and cheerfully, and then turn with eagerness and zest to the things which he can do. Of course, he should never give up too easily. We should always do our best, remembering that we shall have to give account to God for the possibilities he has put into our lives, never wrapping any talent in a napkin, or burying it in the earth. But, after doing our best, it may prove to be with us as it proved to be with Franz Knigstein, that the lofty attainment we had hoped to reach, is beyond our ability and our skill. If so, we should quietly acquiesce, turning to the plainer work which may be given us to do and doing it contentedly.

Many people are made unhappy, by *fretting* over disappointed ambitions. They try to do something conspicuous, to win honor or reward in a certain line, and fail. Then instead of accepting the failure sweetly and taking up the lowlier and less conspicuous tasks cheerfully, they chafe and sometimes lose heart and grow bitter. The way Franz bore himself when he saw that his friend had won the prize was very noble. His disappointment was great. A thousand dreams of success and honor fell into the dust. He saw another wearing the garland, which he had hoped to win and wear. He heard the people's hurrahs and cheers as the other man received the mark of distinction which he himself had hope to receive. Many people in such an experience would have grown bitter and envious, and would have become angry and resentful. But Franz acted nobly. He recognized the splendid ability of Albrecht and honored it. Here it is, that ofttimes *envy* asserts itself and does its mischievous work—but there was not a shadow of envy in the heart of Franz. He was bitterly disappointed—but not an envious word passed his lips. It is one of the finest achievements of a noble spirit, to recognize the genius or the ability that surpasses one's own. It is a heroic and beautiful thing for the boy who has been defeated in the game—to throw up his hat and cheer for his rival. His victory is greater than if he had won in the contest. To master one's own spirit, is the greatest of all victories.

The lesson of the Folded Hands teaches us that if we are not to have the highest place, we should willingly and gladly take the place to which God assigns us. The greatest and most glorious thing anyone can do any day or any hour—is God's will for that day or hour. If that is earth's humblest task, it still is greater for us than if by straying from our true place we should sit on a king's throne a while.

Chapter 18

Comfort for Tired Feet

A good many people come to the close of the day, with tired feet. There are those whose duties require them to walk all the day. There are the men who patrol the city's streets, the guardians of our homes. There are the postmen who bring letters to our doors. There are the messengers who are always hurrying to and fro on their errands. There are the pilgrims who travel on foot along the hard, dusty highways. There are those who follow the plough or perform other parts of the farmer's work. Then there are sales people in the great stores who scarcely ever have an opportunity to sit down. Countless people in factories and mills have the same experience. There are thousands of women in their home work who rarely stop to rest during the long days. Upstairs and down again, from kitchen to nursery, out to the market and to the store, in and out, from early morning until late at night, these busy women are ever plodding in their housewifely duties.

"Man works from sun to sun;
 Woman's work is never done."

No wonder, then, that there are so many sore and tired feet at the end of the day. How welcome night is to the multitudes of weary people, who then drop their tools or their yardsticks or their implements of toil, and hurry home again. How good it is to sit down and rest when the day's tasks are done! There would seem to be need in a lengthy book like this, for a chapter for people with tired feet.

What is the comfort for such? For one thing, there is the though of *duty done*. It is always a comfort, when one is tired—to reflect that one has grown tired in doing one's proper work. A squandered day, a day spent in idleness, may not leave such tired feet in the evening—but neither does it give the sweet pleasure that a busy day gives, even with its blistered and aching feet.

There is a great deal of useless standing or walking, which does not get this comfort. There are young men who stand at the street corners all day and sometimes far into the night, who must have weary feet when at last they turn homeward. Yet they have in their hearts no such compensating satisfaction as those who have toiled all the long hours in some honorable calling. *Idleness* brings only shame and self contempt. Then there are certain kinds of occupation which give to weariness, no sweetening comfort. A day spent in *sinful* work may make the feet tired—but has no soothing for them in the evening's rest.

But all duty well done, has its restful peace of heart when the day's tasks are finished and laid down. Conscience whispers, "You were faithful today; you did all that was given you to do; you did not shirk nor skimp." The *conscience* is the *whisper of God*—and its commendation gives comfort.

But does God really take notice of one's daily, common work—ploughing, delivering letters, selling goods, and cleaning house? Yes! We serve God just as truly in our daily task work, as in our praying and Bible reading. The woman, who keeps the great church clean, sweeping the dust from the aisles, is serving her Lord as well, if her heart is right, as the gorgeously robed minister who performs his sacred part in the holy worship. In one of his poems George Macdonald speaks of standing in a vast church, with its marble floors, worn with knees and feet, and seeing priests flitting among the candles, men coming and going, and then a poor woman with her broom, bowed to her work on the floors, and hearing the Master's voice saying, "Daughter, you sweep well my floor."

The thought that we have done our duty for another day and have pleased God, should always be like soothing balm to our sore and tired feet at the end of the day. The *Master's commendation* takes the *sting* out of any suffering endured in doing even wearisome work for him. When we know that Christ in heaven has noticed our toil, and has approved of it, accepting it as service for himself, we are ready to toil another day.

There is also comfort for tired feet in the coming of night, when one can rest. The day's tasks are finished, the rounds are all made, the errands are all run, the store is closed, the children are in bed, the household work is done—and tired people can sit down and rest. The tight shoes are taken off, loose slippers are substituted, and the evening's quiet begins. Who can tell the blessings that night brings to earth's weary toilers? Suppose there was no night, no rest, that the heavy shoes could never be taken off, that one could never sit down, that there could be no pause in the toil— how wearisome life would be! Night is a holy time, because it brings rest. The rest is all the sweeter, too, because the feet are tired and sore. Those who have never been weary, do not realize the blessings which come with the night.

Wonderful is the work of *repair of the body,* which goes on while we sleep. Men bring the great ships to dock after they have ploughed the waves or battled with the storms and are battered and strained and damaged, and there they repair them and make them ready to go again to sea. At night our jaded and exhausted bodies are dry-docked after the day's conflict and toil, and while we sleep, the mysterious process of restoration and reinvigoration goes on; and when morning comes, we are ready to being a new day of toil and care. We lie down tired, feeling sometimes that we never can do another day's work; but the morning comes again, we rise, renewed in body and spirit, full of enthusiasm, and strong and brave for the hardest tasks.

What a blessing sleep is! It charms away the weariness from the aching limbs; it brushes the clouds from the sky; it refills life's drained fountains. One rendering of the old psalm verse is, "So he gives to his beloved in sleep." Surely God does give us many rich blessings in our sleep. Angels come then with their noiseless tread into our chambers, leave their holy gifts, and steal away unheard. God himself touches us with his benedictions while our eyes are closed in slumber. He shuts our ears to earth's noises and holds us apart from its strifes and turmoil's, while he builds up again in us all that he day has torn down. He makes us forget our griefs and cares, and sends sweet dreams to restore the brightness and the gladness to our tired spirits.

Another comfort for tired feet, is in the thought that Jesus understands the weariness. We know that his feet were tired at the end of many a long day. We are expressly told of one occasion when, being wearied by his long journey, he sat down on a well to rest. He had come far through the dust and the heat, and his feet were sore and weary. All his days were busy days, for he was ever going about on *errands of love.* Many a day he had scarcely time to eat. Though never weary *of,* he was ofttimes weary *in*—his Father's business. When our feet are tired after the day's journeys, it ought to be a very precious comfort, to remember that our blessed Master had like experience, and therefore is able to sympathize with us.

It is one of the chief sadnesses of many lives, that people do not understand them, do not sympathize with them. They move about us—our neighbors and companions, even our closest friends, and laugh and jest and are happy and light-hearted; while we, close beside them, are suffering. They are not aware of our pain, and if they were, they could not give us real sympathy, because they never have had any experience of their own that would interpret to them our experience. Only those who have suffered in some way, can truly sympathize with those who suffer. One who is physically strong, and never has felt the burden of weariness, cannot understand the weakness of another, who, under the least exertion, tires. The man of athletic frame, who can walk all day without fatigue, has small sympathy with the feeble man, who is exhausted in a mile.

When we think of the glory and greatness of Christ, it would seem to us at first that he cannot care for our little ills and sufferings; but when we remember that he once lived on earth, and knows our common life by personal experience, and that he is "touched with the feeling of our infirmities," we know that he understands us and sympathizes with us in every pain. When we think of him sitting weary on a well after his long, hard journey, we are sure that even in heaven he knows what tired feet mean to us, after the day's toil. The comfort even of human sympathy, without any real relief, puts new strength and courage into the heart of one who suffers. The *sympathy of Christ* ought to lift the weary one above all weakness, above all faintness, into victorious joy.

We should remember too, that Christ's feet were tired and hurt—that our feet may be soothed in their pain and weariness, and at last may stand on the golden streets of heaven! There is a legend of Jesus which tells of his walking by the sea, beautiful in his form, wearing brown sandals upon his feet:

"He walked beside the sea; he too his sandals off
To bathe his weary feet in the pure cool wave–
For he had walked across the desert sands
All day long—and as he bathed his feet
He spoke softly to himself, 'Three years! Three years!
And then, poor feet, the cruel nails will come
And make you bleed—but that blood will lave
All weary feet, on all their thorny ways.'"

There is still another comfort for tired feet in the hope of the rest that is waiting. *This incessant toil is not to go on forever!* We are going to a land where the longest journeys will produce no weariness, where "tired feet with sandals loose may rest" from all which tires. The hope of heaven, shining in glory, such a little way before us, ought to give us courage and strength to endure whatever of pain, conflict, and suffering may come to us in those short days.

Chapter 19

The Power of the Risen Lord

The power of the risen Lord began to appear immediately after the resurrection. His death seemed to be the end of everything. While he lived, he had had great power. His ministry was radiant with kindness. His personal influence was felt over all the land. His gracious words as he went about, left benedictions everywhere. He had shown himself sympathetic with all suffering and sorrow. He went about doing good among the people, until he was known everywhere as a man who loved men. His kindness had made him universally beloved. He never wrought a miracle merely to win applause for himself. When in his ministry he did anything supernatural, it was in love and compassion for people. He multiplied the loaves to feed a hungry multitude. He healed blindness, cured the lame and the sick, opened deaf ears—all in sympathy with human distress.

But when he was put to death, his power seemed to end. He was helpless in the hands of his enemies. He was no stronger than the weakest of the land. No hand was lifted for his deliverance. His own strength which had wrought so resistlessly in mighty wonders, gave no sign of power. His name seemed buried in oblivion in the death which he died. Never did any man appear so utterly undone in his death, as did Jesus.

But the moment of his *resurrection*—his power began to show itself. He came from the grave like a God. Those who saw him were strangely impressed by his presence. Without resuming his familiar converse with his friends—he showed himself to them again and again, not in such ways as to awe to bewilder them with the splendors of his glory—but in such simple manifestations as to impress them with the fact of his continued humanness. Mary supposed he was the gardener, so familiar were his form and manner. To the two disciples journeying into the country, he was only a stranger going the same way—but at their simple evening meal, in the breaking of bread—he revealed himself as the risen Christ. To the fishermen on the lake he appeared only as a dim form on the beach—but in the dawn they saw him as the Lord, serving them with love.

Everywhere we see the *power* of the risen Christ. Think of the marvelous power which wrought in the resurrection itself. If the story were merely *legendary* we would have minute details of all the circumstances. The Gospels are "most silent, where myth and legend would be most garrulous." Yet the resurrection was the most stupendous of all the miracles. The world never saw such another exercise of power—as this sublime mastery of death when Jesus came from the grave. All the other of our Lord's miracles were only flashes of power. He changed water into wine. He made the blind to see, the lame to walk, the deaf to hear. A few loaves of bread grew under his hand, until it became abundance for thousands. Other dead were restored—but in every instance they returned again to death. Great as these greatest miracles were, they were little in comparison with this most wonderful of all his acts of power. He rose to die no more!

As soon as Christ arose, *power* began to go forth from him. Think of the change which came upon his friends as soon as they came to believe that their Lord was really alive again. They were transformed men! We know how despairing they were after Jesus died. All their hope was gone. Fear paralyzed them. They hid behind barred doors. But when they saw the hands with the nail prints and believed, they were like new men. The power of the risen Christ passed into them. All who saw them and heard them marveled at their boldness. When we compare the Peter of *Good Friday*, with the Peter of *Pentecost,* we see what the power of the risen Christ made of one man. So it was with all of them. Instead of being feeble, timid men, hiding away in the shadows, following their Master afar off, denying that they belonged to him, locking the doors for fear of assault or arrest, see how bold they became. They feared nothing. They were brave as lions! A tremendous energy was in their words. The power of the risen Christ was upon them. No trust in a *dead* Christ, would have wrought such a marvelous change in those plain, unlettered, untitled men.

The power of the risen Christ is seen in the story of the Christian centuries. Is Christianity the work of a dead leader, a man who was not strong enough to overcome death? Paul tells us that if Christ did not rise there is no Christianity and no hope. "If Christ has not been raised, then is our preaching vain, your faith also is vain; you are you in your sins. Then those also who have fallen asleep in Christ, have perished." If this is the final word about him, there is not a shadow of hope.

But this is not the last word. Rather, it is this, "Christ *has* been raised! He is alive for evermore!" The story of Christianity is the story of the risen Christ. All that has been done he has done. His last promise to his disciples, as he sent them out, was, "Lo, I am with you always, even unto the end of the world." Just what did this promise mean? Is Christ present with his friends in this world in a different way from that in which John or Paul is present in the church? They are present in *influence*. The world is sweeter because John lived in it. He was the apostle of love. There is a fragrance poured out by his name wherever it is spoken. Paul still teaches in all the churches. His words live wherever the New Testament goes. Is it only in this way that Christ's promise must be understood? There are some who tell us this—that he is with his followers only in the memory of his life, work, and character, and not in any sense as a living person, to whom we may speak, who can help us. But the promise meant more than this when Jesus gave it to his friends. It meant that he, the risen Christ, would be with them in actual, living, personal presence, always, all the days—that he would be their Companion, their Helper, and their Friend. The things Christ in his ministry, before his death, "began to do," he has continued to do through all the centuries since. The power of the risen Christ is seen wherever any good work is wrought. We read the wonderful story of his public ministry, how he went everywhere doing good, healing, helping, comforting, and we sometimes wish we could have lived in those days, to have received his help; but the Christ is as really present in our community as he was in Judea and Galilee. We may have his touch, his cheer—his presence, as actually as if he were living in our home.

It is interesting to read of the friendships of the Master, when he was on the earth. He was the friendliest man that ever lived. A recent writer says, "The Son of Man was endowed at birth with impulse and the power to love and minister. His compassion for the multitude because they were distressed and scattered as sheep not having a shepherd; his charity for the outcast, the oppressed, and the weary; his affection for children, are among the tenderest and the sweetest chapters in the history of our race, and seem to have made the profoundest impression both upon those whose exceeding good fortune it was to see his human countenance, and upon the age that came after." If he is the risen Christ, and if he is actually living with us—he is just the same friend to us, that he was to those among whom he lived then. He goes among the people now as he used to do in Galilee. He is the same in our homes of sorrow—as he was in the home of Bethany.

He had his personal friendships. Think what he was to *Peter*—who was brought to him first as Simon, a man of many faults, undisciplined, unlettered, and impetuous. This man of the fishing boats became under his new Master's training and influences, the great apostle. The story of Peter shows what the friendship of Christ can do now with such a man, what it can make of the unlikeliest of us. Or think what the friendship of Christ did for *John*—who grew into such rare gentleness in his companionship, whose character ripened into manly beauty and into great richness and strength. It is possible to have the risen Christ for our friend today— and to have his friendship do for us, just what it did for Peter and John. The power of Christ is seen in Christian lives all over the world, which have been transformed by his love and by his influence.

Easter illustrates the work of the risen Christ in its marvelous power. The day leaves in true Christian hearts everywhere new aspirations, a new uplift of life, new revealing of hope. Easter sends a wave of comfort over the world as it tells of the conquest of death. It changes the mounds above the sleeping dead—into sacred resting places of saints waiting for glory.

But Easter does more. It reaches out and spreads radiance over all sorrow. It tells of victory, not only over death—but over everything in which men seem to suffer defeat—over all grief, pain, and trial. The grain of wheat dies—only that it may live. "If it dies, it bears much fruit." This is the great lesson Christian life. Easter comes on only one day in the year—but it has its lesson for every day. We are continually coming up to graves in which we must lay away some fond hope, some joy—from which the thing laid away rises again in newness of life and beauty.

Every call for *self-denial* is such a grave. Every call to a hard and costly duty is a seed which we bury in the ground—but which will grow into something rich and splendid. "You are called to give up a luxury." Says Phillips Brooks, "and you do it. The little bit of comfortable living is quietly buried away underground. But that is not the last of it. The small indulgence which would have made your bodily life easier for a day or two, undergoes some strange alteration in its burial, and comes out a spiritual quality that blesses and enriches your soul forever."

This is the wider truth of Easter. The only way to do the best and highest—is through the losing of the lower. The rose leaf must be bruised to get its fragrance. Love must suffer, to reveal its full meaning of beauty. The golden grain must be buried in service or sacrifice, that from its grave may rise that which is unseen and eternal.

The secret of all this wondrous truth, is the power of the risen Christ. These things are true—because he died and rose again!

Chapter 20

Coming to the End

We are always coming to the end of something; nothing earthly is long-lived. Many things last but for a day; many, for only a moment. You look at the sunset clouds, and there is a glory in them which thrills your soul; you turn to call a friend to behold the splendor with you—and it has vanished, and a new splendor—as wondrous, though altogether different—is in its place. You cross a field on an early summer morning, and every leaf and every blade of grass is covered with dewdrops, which sparkle like millions of diamonds as the first sunbeams fall on them; but a few moments later you return, and not a dewdrop is to be seen. You walk through your garden today, and note its wondrous variety of flowers in bloom, with their marvelous tints and their exquisite loveliness; tomorrow you walk again along the same paths, and there is just as great variety and as rich beauty—but all is changed.

So it is in all our personal experiences. **Life is a *kaleidoscope*—every moment the view changes.** The beautiful things of one glance are missing at the next, while new things—just as lovely, though not the same—appear in their place. The joys we had yesterday, we do not have today, though our hearts may be quite as happy now, with gladness just as pure and deep. In a sense, to most of us—life is routine, an endless repetition—the same tasks, the same duties, the same cares, day after day, year after year; yet in this routine, there is constant change.

We meet new people, we read new books, we see new pictures, we learn new facts, while at the same time many of the old familiar things are continually dropping out of our lives. The face we saw yesterday—we miss today, and there are new faces in the throng; the songs we sang last year—we do not sing this year; the books we used to read with zest—we do not care for any longer; the pleasures which once delighted us—have no more charm for us; the toys that meant so much to childhood and were so real—have no fascination whatever for manhood and womanhood; the happy days of youth, with their sports and games, their schools and studies, their friendships and visions—are left behind, though never forgotten, as we pass on into actual life with its harder tasks, its rougher paths, its heavier burdens, its deeper studies, its sterner realities. So we are ever coming to the end of old things—and to the beginning of new things. We keep nothing very long.

This is true of our **friendships**. Our hearts are made to love and cling. Very early the little child begins to tie itself to others lives, by the subtle cords of affection. All through life we go on gathering friends and binding them to us by cords of varying strength, sometimes light as a gossamer thread, and as easily broken; sometimes strong as life itself—the very knitting of soul to soul. Yet our friendships are ever changing. Some of them we outgrow and leave behind as we pass from childhood and youth to maturity; some of them have only an external attachment, and easily fall off and are scarcely missed and leave no scar.

In every true life, there is an inner circle of loved ones who are bound to us by ties woven out of our heart's very fibers. The closest of these are the members of our own household. The child's first friend is the child's mother; then comes the father; then the other members of the family are taken into sacred clasp by the opening life. By and by the young heart reaches outside and chooses other friends from the great world of people, and out of the multitude of passing associates, and binds them to itself with friendship's strongest cords. Thus all true men and true women come up to mature years, clustered about by a circle of friends who are as dear to them as their own life.

Our debt to our life's pure and good friendships is incalculable; they make us what we are. *The mother's heart is the child's first school room!* The early home influences, give their tints and hues to the whole afterlife; a gentle home where only kindly words are spoken and loving thoughts and dispositions are nourished, fills with tender beauty—the lives that go out from its shelter. All early friendships print their own stamp on the ripening character. Our souls are like the sensitive plates which the photographer puts into his camera, which catch every image whose reflection falls upon them and hold it ready to be brought out in the finished picture.

True in general, this is especially true of the pure friendships of our lives. None of the impressions that they make on our lives are ever lost; they sink away into our souls—and then reappear at length, in our character.

But even these tender and holy friendships, we cannot keep forever; one by one they fall off or are torn out of our lives. There are many ways of losing friends. Sometimes, without explanation, without offence or a shadow of a reason which we know, without hint or warning given—our friend suddenly withdraws from us and goes his own way, and through life we never have hint or token of the old friendship.

Some friends are lost to us, not by any sudden rupture—but by a slow and gradual falling apart which goes on imperceptibly through long periods, tie after tie unclasping until all are loosed, when hearts once knit together in holy union, find themselves hopelessly estranged. A little bird dropped a seed on a rock. The seed fell into a crevice and grew, and at length the great rock was rent asunder by the root of the tree that sprang up. So *little seeds of alienation* sometimes fall between two friends and in the end produce a separation which rends their friendship and sunders them forever!

Friends are lost, too, through *misunderstanding,* which in many cases a few honest words at first might have removed. The proverb says, "A whisperer separates chief friends."

Friends are lost, too, in the sharp competitions of business, in the keen rivalries of ambition. For love of money or of fame or of power or of special distinction, many throw away holy friendships.

Friends are lost, too, by death. All through life—the sad story of bereavement goes on. As the leaves are torn from the trees by the crude storm, so are friendships plucked from our lives by *Death's remorseless hand.* There is something inexpressibly sad, in the loneliness of old people who have survived the loss of nearly all their friends, and who stand almost entirely alone amid the gathering shadows of their life's eventide. Once they were rich in human affection. Children sat about their table and grew up in their happy home; other true hearts were drawn to them along the years. But one by one, their Christian children are gathered home into God's bosom, until all are gone. Other friends—some in one way and some in another—are also removed. At last the husband or the wife is called away, and one only survives of the once happy pair, lonely and desolate amid the ruin of all earthly gladness, and the tender memories of lost joys.

Were it not for the Christian's hope, these losses of friends along the years would be infinitely sad, without alleviation. But the wonderful grace of God comes not only with its revelation of after life—but with its present healing. God binds up his people's hearts in their sorrow and comforts them in their loneliness. The children and the friends who are gone are not lost; hand will clasp hand again and heart will clasp heart in inseparable reunion. The grave is only *winter*, and after winter comes*spring* with its wonderful resurrections, in which everything beautiful that seemed lost comes again.

We come to the end, also, of many of our life's **visions** and **hopes** as the years go on. Flowers are not the only things which fade. Morning clouds are not the only things which pass away. Sunset splendors are not the only gorgeous pictures which vanish. What comes of all childhood's fancies, of youth's dreams, of manhood's and womanhood's visions and hopes? How many of them are ever realized? Life is full of *illusions*. Many of our ships that we send out to imaginary lands of wealth, to bring back to us rich cargoes—never return at all, or, if they do, only creep back empty, with torn sails and battered hulks. **Disappointments** come to all of us along life's course. Many of our ventures on *life's sea,* are wrecked and never come back to port; many of our ardent hopes, prove only brilliant bubbles which burst as we grasp them!

Yet if we are living for the higher things—the things which are unseen and eternal—then the shattering of our life's dreams, and the failures of our earthly hopes—are only *apparent* losses. The things we can see, are but the shadows of things we cannot see. We chase the shadow, supposing it to be a reality; it eludes us and we do not grasp it! But instead we grasp in our hand that invisible thing of which the visible was only the shadow. A young man has his vision of great achievements and attainments; one by one, with toil and pain, and with quenchless ardor, he follows them. All along his life to its close, bright hopes shine before him, and he continues to press after them with unwearying quest. Perhaps he does not realize any of them, and he comes to old age with empty hands—an unsuccessful man, the world says—but yet all the while his faith in God has not faltered, and he has been gathering into his soul the treasures of spiritual conquest; in his inner life he has been growing richer every day.

Thus, God gives us friends, and our heart's tendrils twine about them; they stay with us for a time, and then leave us. Our loss is very sore, and we go out bereft and lonely, along life's paths. But we have not lost all. Loving our friends drew out to ripeness, the possibilities of love in our own hearts; then the friends were taken away—but the ripened love remains. Our hearts are empty—but our lives are larger. They are but the falling away of the crude scaffolding used in erecting the building, that the beautiful temple itself may stand out in enduring splendor.

We will come to the end of trials and sorrows. Every night has a morning, and, however dark it may be, we have only to wait a little while for the sun to rise, when light will chase away the gloom. Every black cloud which gathers in the sky, and blots out the blue, or hides the stars—passes away before long; and when it is gone there is no stain left on the blue, and not a star's beam is quenched or even dimmed. So it is with life's pains and troubles. *Sickness* gives place to health. *Grief*, however bitter, is comforted by the tender comfort of divine love. *Sorrow*, even the sorest, passes away and joy comes again, not one glad not hushed, its music even enriched by its experience of sadness.

There is another ending—we shall come to the end of **life** itself. We shall come to the close of our last day. We shall do our last piece of work, and take our last walk, and write our last letter, and sing our last song, and speak our last "good night"; then tomorrow we shall be gone, and the palaces which have known us, shall know us no more. Whatever other experiences we may miss—we shall not miss dying. Every human path, through whatever scenes it may wander, must bend at last, into the *Valley of Shadows*.

Yet we ought not to thinks of death as *calamity* or *disaster*; if we are Christians, it will be the brightest day of our whole life—when we are called to go away from earth, and enter heaven. *Work* will then be finished, *conflict* will be left behind— and life in its full, true, rich meaning—will begin.

True *preparation* for death is made when we live each day—as if it were the last. We are never sure of tomorrow; we should leave nothing incomplete any night. Each single, separate little day—should be a miniature life complete in itself—with nothing of duty left over. God gives us life by days, and with each day he gives its own allotment of duty—a portion of his plan to be wrought out, a fragment of his purpose to be accomplished by us. Our mission is to find that bit of divine will— and do it. Well-lived *days*, make completed years; and the well-lived *years* as they come, make a beautiful and full *life*. In such a life, no special preparation of any kind is needed; he who lives thus, is always ready to die. Each day prepares for the next—and the last day prepares for glory!

If we thus live, coming to the end of life need have no terror for us. Dying does not interrupt life for a moment. Death is not a *barrier* cutting off the path—but a *gate* through which passing out of this *world of shadows and unrealities,* we shall find ourselves in the immediate presence of the Lord, and in the midst of the glories of the eternal home.

We need have only one care—that we live well, our one short life as we go on; that we love God and our neighbor; that we believe on Christ and obey his commandments; that we do each duty as it comes to our hand—and do it well. Then no sudden coming to the end will ever surprise us unprepared. Then, while glad to live as long as it may be God's will to leave us here—we shall welcome the gentle angel who comes with great joy, to lead us to out eternal rest and home!

Made in the
USA
Middletown, DE